The Inclusive Education Checklist:

A Self-Assessment of Best Practices

The Inclusive Education Checklist:

A Self-Assessment of Best Practices

by
Richard A. Villa, Ed.D. &
Jacqueline S. Thousand, Ph.D.

DUDE PUBLISHING
A Division of
National Professional Resources, Inc.
www.NPRinc.com

The Inclusive Education Checklist:
A Self-Assessment of Best Practices

Library of Congress Control Number: 2016934545

ISBN 978-1-938539-01-5

PUBLISHING
A Division of:
National Professional Resources, Inc.
Corporate: Katonah, NY
Operations: Naples, FL

For information:
National Professional Resources, Inc.
1455 Rail Head Blvd., Suite 6
Naples, FL 34110
www.NPRinc.com
Toll Free: (800) 453-7461

Cover Design: Jaclyn Falk
Editorial Production: Andrea Cerone
Executive Editor: Lisa Hanson

Contents

Acknowledgments

Shonda S Anderson, M.S. Ed.
Training and Coaching Coordinator, TASN Co-teaching
Kansas Technical Assistance System Network
1020 NE Forest Ave, Topeka, KS 66616
UCP Seguin of Greater Chicago
sanderson@ucpnet.org ~ www/ksdetasn.org/co-teaching

Mary A. Falvey, Ph.D.
Emeriti Professor
Division of Special Education and Counseling
California State University, Los Angeles
mfalvey@calstatela.edu

Beth Gallagher
CEO, Life Works; CEO, Kinship Project
San Diego, CA
bgallagher@lifeworks-sls.com

Lisa Houghtelin
Parent of a child with a disability; Parent Advocate
San Marcos, CA
lhoughtelin@gmail.com

Liz Keefe, Ph.D.
Professor of Special Education
Special Education Department—MSCO5 3040
University of New Mexico
Albuquerque, NM 87131-0001
lkeefe@unm.edu

Ann Nevin, Ph.D.
Professor Emerita
Arizona State University
Ann.nevin@asu.edu

Richard Reid, Ph.D.
Green Mountain Psycho-Educational Services
Jericho, Vermont 05465
gmps@consultant.com

Jodi Robledo, Ph.D.
Assistant Professor, Special Education; Cal-TASH Board Member
College of Education, Health, and Human Services
California State University San Marcos
333 S. Twin Oaks Valley Road
San Marcos, CA 92096
jrobledo@csusm.edu

Richard L. Rosenberg, Ph.D.
Lead Vocational Coordinator, Career Connection
Whittier Union High School District
Part-time Faculty, California State University Los Angeles
9401 S. Painter Ave.
Whittier, CA 90605
Rlrrosenberg@cs.com

Mary Ellen Seaver-Reid, M.Ed. ATP
Educational Consultant, Vermont I-Team/CDCI,
College of Education, Special Education
Faculty, VT LEND, College of Medicine
University of Vermont
Burlington, VT 05401
Mary-Ellen.Seaver-Reid@uvm.edu

Patrick Schwarz, Ph.D.
Professor, Diversity in Learning and Teaching Program
Teacher Preparation
National Louis University, Chicago, IL
PSchwarz@nl.edu

George Theoharis
Professor & Department Chair—Teaching and Leadership
Syracuse University
163 Huntington Hall
Syracuse, New York 13244
gtheohar@syr.edu

Michael Wehmeyer, Ph.D.
Ross and Marianna Beach Professor of Special Education
Director and Senior Scientist, Beach Center on Disability
Director, Kansas University Center on Disability
1200 Sunnyside Avenue, Room 3136
Lawrence, Kansas 66045
wehmeyer@ku.edu

Yazmin Pineda Zapata, Ed.D.
Program Manager/Inclusion Specialist
Health Sciences High and Middle College
3910 University Ave., Suite 100
San Diego, CA 92105
ypineda@hshmc.org

About the Authors

Dr. Richard A. Villa
President, Bayridge Consortium, Inc.
113 West G Street, Suite 444
San Diego, CA 92101
619-795-3602 ~ ravillabayridge@cs.com
www.ravillabayridge.com

Richard A. Villa is President of Bayridge Consortium, Inc. His primary field of expertise is the development of administrative and instructional support systems for educating all students within general education settings. Villa is recognized as an educational leader who motivates and works collaboratively with others to implement current and emerging exemplary educational practices. In the school districts where he has worked and consulted, his efforts have resulted in the inclusion of children with intensive cognitive, physical, and emotional challenges as full members of the general education community. Dr. Villa has been a classroom teacher, special education administrator, pupil personnel services director, and director of instructional services, and has authored seventeen books and more than 100 articles and chapters. Known for his enthusiastic, humorous style, Dr. Villa has presented at international, national, and state educational conferences and has provided technical assistance to departments of education in the United States, Canada, Vietnam, and Honduras and to university personnel, public school systems, and parent and advocacy organizations. Additional information about Dr. Villa can be found at his website, ravillabayridge.com.

Dr. Jacqueline S. Thousand
Professor, California State University San Marcos
333 South Twin Oaks Valley Road, San Marcos, CA 92096
760-533-1744 ~ jthousan@csusm.edu

Jacqueline S. Thousand is a professor in the College of Education, Health, and Human Services of California State University San Marcos, where she designed and coordinated the School of Education's special education professional preparation and master's programs. She previously directed Inclusion Facilitator and Early Childhood/Special Education graduate and postgraduate programs at the University of Vermont and coordinated federal grants concerned with inclusion of students with disabilities in local schools. Dr. Thousand is a nationally known teacher, author, systems change consultant, and disability rights and inclusive education advocate. She is the author of numerous books, research articles, and chapters on issues related to inclusive schooling, organizational change strategies, differentiated instruction and universal design, co-teaching and collaborative teaming, cooperative group learning, creative problem solving, and positive behavioral supports. Dr. Thousand is actively involved in international teacher education and inclusive education endeavors and serves on the editorial boards of several national and international journals.

Introduction —
An Invitation to Invent the Extraordinary

How Was *The Inclusive Education Checklist* Developed?

In this valuable resource, the authors share what they have learned from their over four decades of advocating for and supporting school communities to initiate, implement, and sustain inclusive education best practices for all students. Their experiences that inform the Checklist's content include:

a) Coordination of the U.S. federally funded "Homecoming" project in the early 1980s, which was the first demonstration that students with severe disabilities could be successfully included in general education classrooms in their home neighborhood schools (Thousand, Fox, Reid, Godek, & Williams, 1986);

b) The establishment of one of the first inclusive schools in the United States (Cross & Villa, 1992);

c) The development and delivery of an advanced leadership teacher preparation program to train the first Integration Facilitator educators in the U.S. (Villa & Thousand, 1996);

d) Work with advocacy and educational organizations to establish inclusive education in rural communities, suburban settings, and large urban centers (Thousand et al., 1986; Villa, Falvey, & Shrag, 2003) through statewide systems change efforts in the U.S. (Villa, et al., 2005; Villa & Thousand, 2005); and

e) Teacher training and governmental support of systems change through university affiliations and non-governmental organizations (NGOs) in countries around the world, including Scotland, the Czech Republic, Slovakia, Vietnam, Laos, and

Honduras (McNeil, Villa, & Thousand, 1995; Villa et al., 2003; Villa & Thousand, 2003).

In addition to the authors' experiences, content of *The Inclusive Education Checklist* was shaped by publications, monographs and assessments inclusive of the Vermont Best Practice Statements (Fox & Williams, 1991); the Heterogeneous Education Teacher Survey (Villa, Thousand, Nevin, & Meyers, 1996); the "Starter Kit for Inclusive Education" (Halvorsen, Tweit-Hull, Meinders, Falvey, & Anderson, 2004); the New Mexico "Least Restrictive Environment Assessment and Planning Tool" (Villa, Keefe, Jarry, & Del Rosario, 2003); *Quality Education Practices Assessment* (Villa & Thousand, 2012); and the School Wide Integrated Framework for Transformation (SWIFT) (Sailor & McCart, 2014; Shogren, McCart, Lyon, & Sailor, 2015). Of particular influence were findings of the Working Forum on Inclusive Education (Council for Exceptional Children, 1994), which was convened by the nation's 10 most influential education organizations[1] to identify the characteristics of the nation's first inclusive schools.

Table 1 summarizes these 12 characteristics, which are as important today as when the early innovators in inclusive schooling were studied. *The Inclusive Education Checklist* updates and expands upon these characteristics through a comprehensive and contemporary set of self-assessments.

Finally, the authors sought validation of the content of *The Inclusive Education Checklist* from national disability rights advocates and advocacy organizations, university faculty, teacher trainers, and technical assistance providers with expertise in dimensions of the best practices included in this assessment. The names of the individuals who reviewed and endorsed the Checklist's content appear in the Acknowledgements.

---

[1] These organizations included: American Association of School Administrators, American Federation of Teachers, Council of Great City Schools, National Association of Elementary School Principals, National Association of Secondary School Principals, National Association of State Boards of Education, National Association of State Directors of Special Education, National Education Association, and National School Boards Association.

Table 1.
Characteristics of Inclusive Schools
Identified by the 1994 Working Forum on Inclusive Education

1. *A Sense of Community.* Inclusive schools have a philosophy and a vision that all children belong and can learn in the mainstream of school and community life.

2. *Visionary Leadership.* The administration plays a critical role by articulating the vision, building consensus for the vision, and actively involving and sharing responsibility with the entire school staff in planning and carrying out the strategies that make the school successful.

3. *High Standards.* All children meet high levels of educational outcomes and high standards of performance that are appropriate to their needs.

4. *Collaborative Partnerships.* Students and staff are encouraged to support one another with such strategies as peer tutoring, buddy systems, cooperative learning, co-teaching, teacher-student assistance teams, and other collaborative arrangements.

5. *Changing Roles and Responsibilities.* Teachers lecture less and assist more, school psychologists work more closely with teachers in the classroom, and every person in the building is an active participant in the learning process.

6. *Array of Services.* An array of services are offered that are coordinated with the educational staff and designed to meet the needs of learners experiencing various cognitive, physical, language learning, communication, and/or emotional challenges.

7. *Partnership with Parents.* Parents are embraced as equal and essential partners in the education of their children.

8. *Flexible Learning Environments.* Children are not expected to move in lock step, but rather they follow their own individual paths to learning. Groupings are flexible, and material is presented in concrete, meaningful and differentiated ways that emphasize participation.

continued on next page...

Although there is less reliance on programs that pull children out of classrooms, there are still opportunities for students with and without disabilities to receive separate instruction if needed.

9. ***Strategies Based Upon Research.*** Research into how people learn is providing new ideas and strategies for teachers, and inclusive schools incorporate those ideas. Universal Design for Learning (UDL), differentiated instruction, cooperative learning, constructivist learning theory, culturally relevant and responsive pedagogy, a balanced approached to literacy instruction, interdisciplinary curriculum, authentic assessment of student performance, peer tutoring, direct instruction, reciprocal teaching, learning styles, Multiple Intelligence Theory, social skills training, positive behavior supports, computer-assisted instruction and other forms of technology, and social and study skill training are some of the practices that have emerged from the latest research and are applied in inclusive schools.

10. ***New Forms of Accountability.*** Standardized tests are relied upon less. New forms of accountability and assessment (e.g., portfolios, performance-based assessment) are used to make sure that each student is progressing towards his or her goal(s).

11. ***Access.*** Students have access to the general education curriculum and are able to participate in school life through modifications to buildings and making available appropriate technology.

12. ***Continuing Professional Development.*** An inclusive school enables staff to design and obtain professional development on an ongoing basis.

What Inclusive Education Best Practices Are Assessed in *The Inclusive Education Checklist?*

This book describes and provides best practice indicators for the following 15 inclusive education best practices, which represent a checklist of essential components of quality inclusive education.

☑ 1. Understanding what inclusion is and is not

☑ 2. Home-school-community collaboration

☑ 3. Administrative practices supportive of inclusive education

☑ 4. Redefined roles and responsibilities of general educators; special educators, related services personnel, English language learning and other specialists; and paraeducators

☑ 5. Collaborative planning and creative problem solving for school and post-secondary options

☑ 6. Co-teaching

☑ 7. Student-centered strength-based assessment

☑ 8. Strategies for facilitating access to the general education curriculum

☑ 9. Differentiation of instruction

☑ 10. Student empowerment and natural supports

☑ 11. Multi-Tiered System of Supports (MTSS)/Response to Instruction and Intervention (RtI²)

☑ 12. Positive behavioral supports

☑ 13. Integrated delivery of related services

☑ 14. Transition planning

☑ 15. Site-based continuous planning for sustainability of inclusive education best practices

How to Use *The Inclusive Education Checklist*

The Inclusive Education Checklist is designed to assist schools, districts, administrators, policy makers, community members and professionals interested in education, as well as parents and youth, assess, develop, and implement inclusive services for students with disabilities. For each of the 15 best practices, indicator assessment results offer level of implementation data, which can then be used to plan for continuous program improvement.

The structure of each best practice is as follows. First, the best practice is described. Then, a series of 8 to 32 best practice indicators that deconstruct the best practice is listed, with a place for the rater of the indicators to enter a score in response to the question, "To what degree does this indicator occur in my school?" using the following five-point (i.e., zero to 4) Likert scale and descriptors.

0	1	2	3	4
Never	Rarely	Some of the time	Most of the time	Always

Following each set of best practice indicators is a place to enter the Total Score across items, compute a Mean Score, and indicate the Range (from zero to 4) of responses. For a 10-item set of best practice indicators, this summary would look as follows.

Total Score (out of 40 maximum): _____

Mean Score (Total Score/10): _____

Range of Scores: _____ (low) to _____ (high)

The Mean Score can be computed for an individual respondent, a subgroup of the school population (e.g., parents, special educators and specialists, related service personnel, general educators) or aggregated across all respondents. The Mean Score offers a general indicator of the degree to which elements of a best practice are currently being implemented and can be used as a general indicator of school progress toward achieving the best practice.

Using a scale such as the one below, a Mean Score can be used to signal both general school "health" regarding a best practice, as well as the degree of need or urgency to work on that best practice. For example, a best practice Mean Score of 2.0 might suggest that a school is "in need of considerable improvement," whereas a Mean Score of 2.6 might suggest that a school is "on its way," yet still in need of considerable improvement.

Progress Toward Best Practice Excellence
(as Indicated by Mean Score)

0 – 1.0	1.1 – 2.0	2.1 – 3.0	3.1 – 4.0
Need to start	Need considerable improvement	On our way	Doing well

The Range of Scores data offer another metric that reflects the variability of implementation and quality within a particular best practice area. For example, a Mean Score of 2.5 might represent a narrow Range of Scores from 2 to 3 (e.g., representing five "most of the time" and five "some of the time" scores). A narrower range might suggest the need for a general course of action, such as a school-wide professional development and support initiative. A Mean Score of 2.5 could also represent a wide Range of Scores from 0 to 4 (representing "never" to "always" ratings). A wider range of ratings might suggest the need to target the "never" and "rarely" indicators as priority areas of improvement.

Inclusive Education Best Practice #1:

Understanding What Inclusion Is and Is Not

The authors are fond of the saying, "Half of knowing what something *is*, is knowing what it is *not*." So, in defining inclusive education, we choose to define it in terms of both what it is and what it is not. We end with a summary of the research supporting inclusive education.

Inclusive Education is NOT

*Inclusive education is **not** mainstreaming.* In the mainstreaming movement of the 1970s, students with disabilities were only present in classes where they could pretty much do what everybody else could do. Mainstreaming primarily applied to students with mild disabilities (i.e., students with learning disabilities and/or those eligible for speech and language services). The focus was on a child being "ready" to learn rather than the school being ready to support diverse learners. There was not much differentiation of instruction or in-class support provided by special educators or general education teachers. Thus, many general education teachers perceived that students with disabilities were "dumped" into their classrooms without any support to them or the student(s). For many students, mainstreaming resulted in being in general education only for related arts classes (e.g., art, music, physical education), lunch and recess, or being placed in classrooms with younger rather than same-aged peers.

*Inclusive education also is **not** integration.* The integration movement of the 1980s expanded the discussion of who could and should belong in general education beyond students with mild disabilities to students with moderate and severe disabilities. Integration, however, focused primarily on physical and social access, with limited or no academic expectations for students with moderate and severe disabilities.

Finally, *inclusive education is **not** routinely or automatically grouping students* with disabilities and other students perceived as low performing or educationally or behaviorally challenging in *homogeneous* tiered and leveled groups for instruction, particularly in high-stakes content and assessment areas such as literacy and mathematics. Homogeneous grouping is appropriate and essential for targeted intervention and short-term remediation, as long as the groupings are fluid, flexible, and based upon ongoing data collection and analysis. The bottom line is that in inclusive education students are primarily grouped in *heterogeneous mixed-ability* groups during the day, week and year.

Inclusive Education IS

*Inclusive education **is** both a vision and a practice.* Namely, *inclusive education is* both the *vision and practice* of welcoming, valuing, empowering, and supporting the diverse academic, social/emotional, language, and communication learning of all students in shared environments and experiences for the purpose of attaining the desired goals of education. Inclusion is a *belief* that everyone belongs, regardless of need or perceived ability, and that all are valued and contributing members of the school community.

*Inclusive education also **is** the practice* of differentiating instruction for students through collaborative planning and teaching among all members of the school community, including students and families. It *is* providing all students with instruction in and opportunities to practice self-determination (choice making) in learning and goal setting.

*Inclusive education **is** presumed competence.* For all students, including students with more extensive support needs (historically referred to as students with moderate and severe disabilities), *inclusive education is* presuming competence and holding the highest of expectations (National Alternate Assessment Center, 2006) by creating *"personally meaningful curriculum"* (Bambara, Koger, Burns, & Singley, 2016, p. 475) that blends opportunities to acquire academic and functional knowledge and skills within the context of general education and natural routines, "with decisions about 'what to teach when and where' driven by family and individual preferences, values, and vision" (Bambara et al., 2016, p. 475).

Biklen and Burke (2006) recognize a "tradition in American education to assume incompetence of students who have severe communication impairments...through the process of classification" (p. 166). They point out that each of us has a choice to presume a person with significant disabilities to be incompetent, or "admit that one cannot know another's thinking unless the other can reveal it. The latter... more conservative choice... refuses to limit opportunity by *presuming competence*" (p. 166). Presumption of competence in the absence of evidence to the contrary is not a new notion. In the early 1980s, Donnellan and Leary (1984) described the notion of presumed competence, naming it the criterion of least dangerous assumption.

Summarizing, Jorgensen (2005) writes, "the least-dangerous assumption when working with students with significant disabilities is to assume that they are competent and able to learn, because to do otherwise would result in harm such as fewer educational opportunities, inferior literacy instruction, a segregated education, and fewer choices as an adult" (p. 5). The most dangerous assumption is to fail to presume competence, intelligence, and potential for growth. The criterion of least dangerous assumption is the *presumption of competence at all times for all persons.*

Inclusive education is supported by research . As early as the 1980s, research showed that separate special education services had little to no positive effects for students, regardless of the intensity or type of their disability (Lipsky & Gartner, 1989). In a meta-analysis of effective special education settings, Baker,

Wang, and Wahlberg (1994), concluded, "special-needs students educated in regular classes do better academically and socially than comparable students in non-inclusive settings" (p. 34). This held true regardless of the type of disability or grade level of the student.

In 1995, the U.S. Department of Education reported that "across a number of analyses of post-school results, the message was the same: those who spent more time in regular education experienced better results after high school" (p. 87). In 2005, Blackorby and colleagues' study of 11,000 students with disabilities found that those who spent more time in general education classrooms were absent less, performed closer to grade level than their peers in pullout settings, and had higher achievement test scores. The study confirmed that students with disabilities in general education settings academically outperformed their peers in separate settings when standards-based assessments were used. As for the impact of inclusive education on the learning of other students in the class, Kalambouga, Farrell, & Dyson's 2007 meta-analysis found that 81% of the outcomes reported showed that including students with disabilities resulted in either positive or neutral effects for students without disabilities. As for students with more extensive support needs, researchers found that their inclusion did not adversely affect classmates' academic or behavioral success as measured by standardized tests and report card grades. They also found that their inclusion enhanced classmates' as well as their own achievement, self-esteem, and school attendance (Kelly, 1992; Straub & Peck, 1994).

Overall, the data speak volumes. Students with disabilities acquire greater mastery of academic and social content in inclusive settings. In summary, as federal legislation acknowledges in the Individuals with Disabilities Education Improvement Act (IDEIA) of 2004, "nearly 30 years of research and experience has demonstrated that the education of children with disabilities can be made more effective by having high expectations and ensuring students' access in the general education curriculum to the maximum extent possible.... [and] providing appropriate special education and related services and aides and supports in the regular classroom to such children, whenever possible" (20 U.S.C. 1400(c)(5)).

Inclusion is a Journey

Currently, 61% of students with disabilities spend 80% or more of their day in general education settings (Snyder and Dillow, 2015). Where does the "80% or more of the day" statement come from? Data reported annually to the U.S. Office of Special Education and Rehabilitative Services (OSERS) is analyzed to determine the percentage of students ages 6 through 21 who are educated inside the regular class 80% or more of the day, between 40% and 79% of the day, and less than 40% of the day. A day is defined as the entire school day inclusive of lunch, recess, study periods, and specials such as art, physical education and music. These data are made public in an annual OSERS report to the U.S Congress (OSERS, 2014).

Ideally, the goal of inclusive education is for nearly 100% of students with disabilities to be educated within general education nearly 100% of the school day. Current national data (i.e., 61% of students educated in general education classrooms for 80% or more of the day) suggest that many schools have a distance to go in their journey to achieving this ideal. Why? Some school systems have yet to attempt or achieve community consensus for an inclusive vision. Some schools have yet to orchestrate the structural supports (e.g., co-teaching, master schedules that allow for collaborative planning) to make it happen easily. Some schools have yet to provide their school personnel with the training in how to meet diverse student needs in mixed-ability classrooms. Some schools have not yet had the opportunity to educate their students with more pervasive and intensive support needs, who are still being educated in segregated classrooms and schools, in general education classrooms. Finally, there are those few students for whom general education, 100% of the day, does not best support their momentary needs or goals (e.g., students who are hospitalized, secondary students engaged in job development in the community for part of the school day). It is for these reasons that we do not identify 100% as the target for the best practices indicator items 13 and 14.

Indicator 13 targets at least 90% (rather than 61%) of students with IEPs having general education as a primary educational placement. Why set a target of 90%, when the national average is 61%? Because national averages are just that, a central tendency measure representing schools performing both below and above the mean. Averages factor in the fact that there *are* states, districts, and individual schools across the nation that *do* exceed the mean and, in some cases, are known (by the authors and this book's endorsers) to have approached and hit the suggested targets. Since this is a *best practice* indicator, we chose a target that substantially exceeds the national average, yet is within reach.

Indicator 14 targets at least 80% of students with IEPs receiving instruction in *core academic content* in general education classrooms (in the best case scenario with special education support through co-teaching) rather than in segregated content classes. Why set an 80% target? Unlike for Indicator 13, there are no federal or state data indicating the proportion of students with IEPs receiving or *not* receiving academic content instruction from credentialed general education content experts in general education content courses (i.e., language arts, mathematics, science, social studies) or classrooms. However, the authors and those who endorsed this book know of a substantial number of students with more intensive support needs who receive little *academic content instruction* at all, in either special or general education settings. We also know of a substantial number of secondary students who receive their *academic content instruction* in replacement content classes populated only by students with IEPs rather than in general education classes taught by credentialed content experts. The lower 80% standard for Indicator 14 acknowledges this reality, yet sets a substantial performance target for the indicator.

As a final comment, we anticipate that target percentages for these and other indicators should and will rise over time. As we do better, we can set out sights higher — on even more ambitious targets. It is our hope that the use of this best practice assessment tool and its indicators will facilitate the day when the ideal becomes the reality for all children with disabilities, their families, and the educators responsible for their education.

Inclusive Education
Best Practice Checklist Assessment

Inclusive Education Best Practice #1:
Understanding What
Inclusion Is and Is Not

<u>Directions</u>: Based upon your experience, please give each of the following 15 indicators a (zero to 4) rating in response to the question, "To what degree does this indicator occur in my school?"

0	1	2	3	4
Never	Rarely	Some of the time	Most of the time	Always

Rating (0 – 4)	Indicator of Understanding What Inclusion Is And What It Is Not
	1. Students with disabilities attend the *home school* or *school of choice* they would attend if they did not have an Individual Education Program (IEP).
	2. The *length of the school day* for students with disabilities is *not shorter* than the length of the school day for same-aged classmates without disabilities.
	3. The *placement option of first choice* discussed for each child with a disability is the general education classroom with the provision of any necessary supplemental supports, aids, and services. The presumption is that the student is educated with his/her non-disabled peers with the provision of specially-designed instruction (special education services), supplementary aids and services, and related services.
	4. Students with disabilities are educated *alongside peers* who are at or near the same *chronological age*.
	5. All students with disabilities have access to the *same curricular and co-curricular* (before and after school)

Rating (0 – 4)	Indicator of Understanding What Inclusion Is And What It Is Not

activities as their non-disabled peers. (Note: The Individuals with Disabilities Education Improvement Act (IDEIA) of 2004 defines the general education curriculum as the sum total of all experiences, inclusive of co-curricular activities, made available to non-disabled students.)

6. *Person-first language* is used when describing students. When describing a student, ability is emphasized (e.g., "uses a communication device" rather than "unable to speak"); and the person is put first, before the disability (e.g., "a child with Down syndrome" rather than the "Down's student"). We do not refer to students by categorical labels or program name (e.g., special class students, sped kids, Center kid, ELLs).

7. Staff (educators, administrators, paraeducators) *presume competence* for all students, especially students with difficulties in communicating and those with significant disabilities. (Please see the **Inclusive Education Is Presumed Competence** section in the preceding narrative for the meaning of presumed competence as used in this indicator.)

8. General education teachers are provided with and use specific information regarding each student's *strengths* (e.g., learning styles, Multiple Intelligences, hobbies, interests) and *needs* (e.g., academic, social-emotional, communication, language goals) in order to facilitate and support each student to reach his or her potential.

9. Lack of *adequate personnel or resources* is NOT used to argue that a student with a disability should be removed from general education.

10. The *need for modifications* to the general education curriculum is NOT used to argue that a student with a disability should be removed from general education.

Rating (0 – 4)	Indicator of Understanding What Inclusion Is And What It Is Not

☐ 11. All student *subgroups* (e.g., English language learners, students eligible for special education services, children in poverty) are achieving mastery as demonstrated by each subgroup making expected progress (e.g., one month gain from a month of instruction).

☐ 12. Students are supported to learn skills leading to greater *independence, self-determination,* and *self-advocacy.* This occurs through students participating as

   a) instructors for themselves (e.g., independent learners) and others (e.g., members of cooperative learning groups, peer tutors, co-teachers);

   b) advocates for themselves and others (e.g., participating on IEP teams brainstorming accommodations and modifications); and

   c) decision makers (e.g., determining school and classroom rules, participating on school committees, student-led parent-teacher conferences, student-led IEP and transition meetings).

☐ 13. Across all 13 federal special education eligibility categories[2] and racial/ethnic groups, *90% or more* of students with disabilities are *educated within general education classes* for 80% or more of the school day. (Please see the explanation for these target percentages in the *Inclusive Education is a Journey* section of the preceding narrative.)

---

[2] The Individual with Disabilities Educational Improvement Act (IDEIA) of 2004 identifies 13 different disability categories under which students ages 3 through 21 may be eligible for special education services: autism, deaf-blindness, deafness, emotional disturbance, hearing impairment, intellectual disability, multiple disabilities, orthopedic impairment, other health impairment, specific learning disability, speech or language impairment, traumatic brain injury, and visual impairment.

Rating   Indicator of Understanding What
(0 – 4)   Inclusion Is And What It Is Not

☐   14. Across all 13 federal special education eligibility
categories and racial/ethnic groups, *80% or more* of
students with disabilities receive their instruction in
core academic curriculum (i.e., language arts, mathematics, science, social studies) in *general education
academic classes* rather than in alternative special
education content classes. (Please see the explanation
for this target percentage in the ***Inclusive Education is
a Journey*** section of the preceding narrative.)

☐   15. The percentage of students in the school eligible for
special education *mirrors and does not exceed* the
national, state, or regional percentage. Note: According
to the National Center for Educational Statistics in
the most recently reported school year, just under 13%
of children ages 3 to 21 were served under IDEIA.
National percentages vary from year to year, as do state
and regional percentages, depending upon population
demographics, state-specific eligibility criteria, and other
factors such as public health changes (e.g., increases in
children with asthma and health impairments).

Total Score (out of 60 maximum):   _____

Mean Score (Total Score/15):   _____

Range of Scores: _____ **(low) to**   _____ **(high)**

Inclusive Education Best Practice #2:
Home-School-Community Collaboration

The importance of parent and family engagement to student success has been long documented (National Center on School Restructuring and Inclusion, 1996). The U.S. Congress recognized the power of parent participation in the findings of the 2004 reauthorization of The Individuals with Disabilities Education Act (IDEA), acknowledging that, "nearly 30 years of research and experience has demonstrated that the education of children with disabilities can be made more effective by strengthening the role of parents and ensuring that families of such children have meaningful opportunities to participate in the education of their children" (IDEIA, 2004).

Families are the building blocks of society and the constant in the lives of their sons and daughters. Therefore, educators are obliged to provide opportunities for families to participate as integral partners in the development and implementation of their children's Individual Education Programs (IEPs). Educators and students can only benefit from doing everything possible to facilitate family engagement in the educational process and *home-school collaboration*. For example, family involvement in the IEP process is one of the best ways to ensure that student goals are implemented not only at school, but in a student's home and community.

Schools, students, and families also benefit from the establishment of *school-community* collaborations. Schools that organize partnerships with local businesses, public service agencies, private foundations, volunteer organizations, YMCAs and other youth organizations, university teacher preparation programs, and other service-oriented organizations both expand the potential services available to their students and create opportunities for family members to become involved in school and community activities.

Inclusive Education
Best Practice Checklist Assessment

Inclusive Education Best Practice #2:
Home-School-Community Collaboration

Directions: Based upon your experience, please give each of the following 12 indicators a (zero to 4) rating in response to the question, "To what degree does this indicator occur in my school?"

0	1	2	3	4
Never	Rarely	Some of the time	Most of the time	Always

Rating (0 – 4)	Indicator of Home-School-Community Collaboration
☐	1. Families have frequent opportunities to *visit* their child's *classroom*.
☐	2. Teachers and administrators *welcome* families into *decision-making processes* for student achievement and instruction.
☐	3. Established *structures and procedures* (e.g., holding meetings at times when family members can attend, home visits) facilitate *communication* between families and teachers not only at IEP meetings but on an *ongoing basis* throughout the year.
☐	4. Families of children with IEPs are *included* in all invitations to *school-based functions* and volunteer/service opportunities.
☐	5. Families, educators, related service personnel, and students *collaborate* in *writing IEP goals*.
☐	6. Families and students are a) *informed* of their *due process and procedural safeguards* and their *rights* regarding *confidentiality* of student records, b) provided *clear information* about whom to contact and what *steps*

Rating (0 – 4)	Indicator of Home-School-Community Collaboration

to take when they have an educational concern, and c) offered r*eady access* to records they seek in a manner consistent with district policies and procedures.

7. School personnel *maintain confidentiality* with respect to information about students with IEPs and their families. *Only* school personnel with a *legitimate inter-est* in the education of a student with an IEP *have access* to that student's records.

8. When school policies and procedures are updated, *input* is *solicited* from *family members, community partners,* and *students* as well as staff.

9. School personnel solicit and *consider family* members' *perspectives* regarding their child's strengths, interests, and learning preferences when making IEP-related decisions.

10. School-based parent-teacher associations, site improvement councils, and other similar *decision-making and advisory groups* have a *designated position* for a family member of a child with an IEP.

11. The school collaborates with a variety of *community partners* (e.g., businesses, public service agencies, private foundations, volunteer organizations, youth organizations, universities, service-oriented organizations) *to expand* community *resources* and services to meet school and student needs.

12. The school *connects families* of students with IEPs with *community resources* and partnerships relevant to family support interests and needs.

Total Score (out of 48 maximum): _____

Mean Score (Total Score/12): _____

Range of Scores: _____ **(low) to** _____ **(high)**

Inclusive Education Best Practice #3:

Administrative Practices Supportive of Inclusive Education

Administrative leadership and support is central to achieving the beneficial outcomes of inclusive education. What does administrative leadership look like and sound like? It looks and sounds like principals, district office personnel, grade-level and departmental team leaders, and special education directors taking the lead in *articulating and building consensus for an inclusive vision* of all students being welcomed, valued, empowered, and supported in learning academic, social-emotional, language, and communication skills in shared environments and experiences. It sounds like administrators clarifying for school staff how inclusive education relates to and supports other best practice initiatives, such as co-teaching among general and special educators and implementing Career and College Readiness Standards and a Multi-Tiered System of Supports (MTSS) for academic and behavioral success (Villa & Thousand, 2011). It looks like master schedules arranged so that teachers and other school personnel can collaborate in planning and teaching.

Administrative leadership also looks and sounds like *systematic professional development* that includes coaching and mentorship so that educators learn and practice skills in collaborative planning and teaching skills (e.g., co-teaching) and differentiated instruction for students with and without IEPs. Administrative leadership looks and sounds like the crafting and delivery of meaningful *incentives* to encourage educators to learn and use new instructional and behavior support approaches. Administrative leadership looks like the *reorganization of human resources* to eliminate redundancies and encourage shared responsibility among all personnel for all students. Finally, administrative leadership looks and sounds like moving people through a systematic and transparent *action planning* and implementation process regarding vision, skills, resources and incentives so that inclusive education practices occur with integrity.

Inclusive Education
Best Practice Checklist Assessment

Inclusive Education Best Practice #3:
Administrative Practices
Supportive of Inclusive Education

<u>Directions</u>: Based upon your experience, please give each of the following 18 indicators a (zero to 4) rating in response to the question, "To what degree does this indicator occur in my school?"

0	1	2	3	4
Never	Rarely	Some of the time	Most of the time	Always

Rating (0 – 4) | **Indicator of Administrative Practices Supportive of Inclusive Education**

1. In order to effect *continuous improvement* in instruction and address the learning of all students, the school has and uses an effective schoolwide *Multitiered System of Supports* (MTSS) and/or *Response to Instruction and Intervention* (RtI^2) approach of universal screening, universal access to high quality instruction across content areas, multiple tiers of intervention, data-driven decision making, and problem-solving teaming.

2. Building-level administrators *regularly and publicly convey a commitment to and rationale for inclusive education* and the practices that support it (e.g., collaborative planning, co-teaching, creative problem solving, collaboration with families, differentiated instruction, MTSS/RtI^2). Administrators make explicit connections between inclusion and the school's ongoing improvement initiatives and the school's over-arching vision, mission, and goals for all students.

Rating   Indicator of Administrative Practices
(0 – 4)   Supportive of Inclusive Education

☐   3.   *Professional Learning Communities* (PLCs) are established and used to provide forums in which educators can practice problem solving for students, analyze student data, and plan for co-teaching and differentiation.

☐   4.   Least Restrictive Environment (LRE) mandates and inclusive practices (e.g., provision of accommodations and modifications, collaboration in planning and teaching) are included and addressed in *teacher evaluations*.

☐   5.   Building *administrators* work with district personnel to ensure that *all* students, including those who receive specially designed instruction (i.e., have IEPs) and English language development services, have *access to* the *general education curriculum,* including textbooks and other instructional materials, supplies, assistive technology, and transportation.

☐   6.   Students who receive specially designed instruction (i.e., have IEPs) and English language development services have access to the *co-curricular* (after-school and before-school non-academic) activities available to other students without support needs.

☐   7.   *Staff roles have been redefined* so that everyone is expected to a) educate the diverse group of learners in the school and b) participate in MTSS/ RtI^2 collaborative planning and problem solving, differentiation of instruction, and co-teaching.

☐   8.   Administrators systematically *determine the collaboration needs* of school personnel. (E.g., With whom do various staff need to collaborate? For what purposes? How often?).

☐   9.   The *master schedule* is designed to allow *time for planning* and teaching among school personnel who need to collaborate.

Rating (0 - 4)	Indicator of Administrative Practices Supportive of Inclusive Education

☐   10. Collaborators (e.g., special and general educators who co-teach) are periodically and regularly *provided with extra time* (e.g., release time, in-service time) to *collaboratively plan* and problem solve.

☐   11. In addition to planning time, the administration provides *incentives* (e.g., recognition for efforts and accomplishments of collaborators, provision of coaching, provision of release time to observe one another in action, sending teams to conferences, teams asked to make presentations about their accomplishments) *for collaborative planning* and problem solving.

☐   12. *School and community members are kept apprised* (e.g. via website, newsletters, reports, presentations to the school board) of the *accomplishments* of problem solving, MTSS/RtI², differentiation, and co-teaching teams.

☐   13. *Staff development* (e.g., workshops, courses, mentoring and peer coaching, Professional Learning Communities (PLCs), book studies, job shadowing, pairing of new collaborating and teaching teams with veteran collaborators) to create common conceptual language and frameworks, skills, and dispositions has occurred and is ongoing.

☐   14. Within the past two years, high-quality *professional development in inclusive education* (e.g., what it is, what is not, the research supporting inclusion—see **Best Practice #1**) has been provided to all *school personnel.*

☐   15. Within the past two years, high-quality *professional development* in the elements of a Multi-Tiered System of Supports (MTSS) and/or Response to Instruction and Intervention (RtI²) has been provided to all school personnel.

Rating   **Indicator of Administrative Practices**
(0 – 4)   **Supportive of Inclusive Education**

☐ 16. Within the past two years, high-quality *professional development* in *differentiated instruction* has been provided to all school personnel.

☐ 17. Within the past two years, high-quality *professional development in collaborative planning, creative problem solving,* and *family-school collaboration* has been provided to all school personnel.

☐ 18. Within the past two years, high-quality *professional development* in *co-teaching* has been provided to school personnel.

Total Score (out of 72 maximum): _____

Mean Score (Total Score/18): _____

Range of Scores: _____ (low) to _____ (high)

Inclusive Education
Best Practice #4:
Redefined Roles And Responsibilities

Resources in education may be *technical* and *material* (e.g., computer hardware and software, curriculum materials), *organizational* (e.g., how the school day, week, and year and the people in the organization are arranged; time is structured so staff can collaborate), or *human*. Human resources are the adults (school personnel, family, and community members) and students and their unique gifts, talents, and traits. It can be argued that human resources are the most important to school health and the success of inclusive education.

The change in the role of administrators of an inclusive school was examined and assessed by the indicators in **Inclusive Best Practice #3**. The school administrator is not the only human resource role that morphs in inclusive schooling. Most, if not all, *human resource roles shift*. Distinct professional titles (i.e., general versus special educator) may be dropped. Traditional job functions may be redistributed and shared among instructional personnel, so that collaboration in planning, teaching, and assessment become common explicitly-stated job functions. Employees are educated on the shift in their respective roles to support students with IEPs to be academically, physically, and socially included. Everyone is a participant in professional development that clarifies their interdependent roles and builds their capacity to collaborate with one another and educate a heterogeneous student body in mixed-ability classrooms.

The indicators for Best Practice #4 represent the redefined roles and job responsibilities of general educators, specialists, paraeducators, and other support and health personnel working in inclusive schools.

Inclusive Education
Best Practice Checklist Assessment

Inclusive Education Best Practice #4:
Redefined Roles And Responsibilities

Directions: Based upon your experience, please give each of the following 32 indicators a (zero to 4) rating in response to the question, "To what degree does this indicator occur in my school?"

0	1	2	3	4
Never	Rarely	Some of the time	Most of the time	Always

Rating   Indicator of Redefined Roles and Responsibilities
(0 – 4)

TO BE COMPLETED BY GENERAL EDUCATORS
Directions for rating: Please rate each item using the following sentence starter:
"In my school, general educators..."

1. *...have ownership for and assume primary responsibility for ensuring that EVERY student in their classrooms,* including students with disabilities and students learning English, actively participates in instructional activities in meaningful ways.

2. *...actively participate in IEP meetings* for students with disabilities, other students who struggle in learning, and students learning English.

3. *...*actively participate with special education teachers, related services personnel (e.g., speech and language pathologist), English language learning specialists, and others to *collaboratively plan for differentiated instruction in their classrooms and to collaboratively evaluate* student success.

4. *...*work collaboratively with special educators and others to *identify and implement specific curricular adaptations and instructional strategies* needed by

Rating   **Indicator of Redefined Roles and Responsibilities**
(0 – 4)

---

students with disabilities, other students who struggle in learning, and students learning English.

☐   5.   ...work with others to *train and supervise paraeducators* assigned to their classes to provide learning support to students with disabilities, other students who struggle in learning, and students learning English.

☐   6.   ...*co-teach* with special educators, intervention specialists, and others to facilitate student access to the content being taught in their classes.

☐   7.   ...utilize *evidence-based practices* such as cooperative group learning, peer tutoring, active learning, and differentiated instruction to support meaningful inclusive education.

☐   8.   ...facilitate *positive relationships* among all students in their classrooms.

☐   9.   ...work collaboratively with special educators and English language learning specialists when *assigning grades* and administering and interpreting other assessment/evaluation data for students on their caseloads.

☐   10. ...work collaboratively with others to *keep families regularly informed of student progress,* including the progress of students with disabilities and English learners.

TO BE COMPLETED BY SPECIAL EDUCATORS, RELATED SERVICES PERSONNEL, ELL AND OTHER SPECIALISTS
Special Note: Rather than scoring each role separately, provide a rating that best represents how specialists typically practice their roles in your school.
Directions for rating: Please rate each item using the following sentence starter:
   "In my school, special educators and other specialists..."

☐   11. ...*schedule, actively participate in, and facilitate* meetings for students with disabilities, students learning English, and students who otherwise need

Rating **Indicator of Redefined Roles and Responsibilities**
(0 – 4)

---

differentiated learning, behavior, and/or social-emotional support.

☐ 12. ...actively participate with general education teachers and others in collaborative planning, instruction, and evaluating *progress in the curriculum and language development* of students with disabilities and students learning English.

☐ 13. ...work collaboratively with others to ensure that *IEP goals and English language development needs are addressed in students' daily schedules.*

☐ 14. ...work collaboratively with general educators and others to *identify and implement specific curricular adaptations and instructional strategies* needed by students with disabilities and English learners.

☐ 15. ...work with others to *train, direct and supervise* para-educators assigned to provide students with disabilities needed supports in general education classrooms.

☐ 16. ...*model* for general educators and paraeducators methods and strategies for supporting students with disabilities in general education settings (e.g., facilitate peer-to-peer support, independence).

☐ 17. ...*co-teach* with general educators and others to facilitate access to the content in general education classes.

☐ 18. ...use *evidence-based practices* such as cooperative group learning, peer tutoring, active learning, and differentiated instruction to support meaningful inclusive education.

☐ 19. ...*pre-teach* or *re-teach* content to students, when necessary.

☐ 20. ...facilitate *positive relationships among all students* (e.g., provide social skills instruction, conduct class

Rating (0 – 4)	Indicator of Redefined Roles and Responsibilities

meetings, teach cooperative group lessons that focus upon social as well as academic skills, facilitate Circle of Friends) to promote genuine social inclusion.

21. …work collaboratively with general educators when *assigning grades* and administering and interpreting other assessments/evaluations for students on their caseloads.

22. …*regularly monitor* and report progress of goal attainment for students with IEPs, English learners, and others who receive their services.

23. …work collaboratively with others to *keep families regularly informed of student progress* for students with disabilities, English learners, and students in other support programs (e.g., Title 1, gifted and talented).

24. …work collaboratively with others to *plan for transitions* to facilitate students' movement from grade to grade, to a new school, and beyond high school.

TO BE COMPLETED BY PARAEDUCATORS

Directions for rating: Please rate each item using the following sentence starter:
   "In my school, paraeducators (paraprofessionals, instructional assistants)…"

25. …*work under the direction and supervision* of classroom teachers, special educators, and/or other specialists.

26. …have opportunities to *communicate and collaboratively plan* with and/or *receive training* or modeling from their supervisors on a weekly basis.

27. …are *actively engaged in instruction or monitoring* students as students work independently, with partners, or in groups.

Rating   **Indicator of Redefined Roles and Responsibilities**
(0 – 4)

☐	28. …support students with disabilities and English learners (as well as all students) in *general education classrooms to implement specific curricular adaptations and instructional strategies* identified as needed to progress in the general education curriculum.
☐	29. …interact with students in ways that *build positive relationships* among peers in academic and non-academic activities (e.g., facilitate natural peer supports, problem solving).
☐	30. …facilitate student *independence* and *natural peer supports* by avoiding being "velcroed" to (e.g., sitting next to and interacting only with) "assigned" students or students with identified special needs.
☐	31. …*support classroom teachers* and *any students* in a general education classroom (not just students with IEPs or other identified support needs, such as English learners), as needed.
☐	32. …*collect data* on student progress on academic, behavior, communication, language or other goals, as needed or directed.

Total Score (out of 125 maximum):   _____

Mean Score (Total Score/32):   _____

Range of Scores: _____ (low) to   _____ (high)

Inclusive Education
Best Practice #5:
Collaborative Planning and Creative Problem Solving

5

Key to successful inclusive education are opportunities to develop and practice effective and efficient collaborative teaming skills. In a national study of over 600 general and special education teachers and administrators, Villa, Thousand, Nevin, and Meyers (1996) found collaboration to be one of the top three predicators (along with administrative support and professional development) of positive attitudes toward inclusive education. Likewise, the National Center on Educational Restructuring and Inclusion (1995, 1996) found opportunities for personnel to collaborate (i.e., building-level planning teams, scheduled time for teachers to plan and teach together, effective collaboration with parents) critical to successful inclusion.

A variety of collaborative teams exist within schools, based upon the team's defined function. Individual Education Program (IEP) planning teams exist for students eligible for special education. Most every school has a general education problem-solving team. This team goes by various names—Student Study Team, Student Success Team, MTSS/RtI team—but the function of the team is the same: to support classroom teachers, problem solve issues with individual students, and prevent unnecessary referral for assessment for special education eligibility. Positive Behavior

Support, Professional Development, and Professional Learning Community teams are other common school-based teams.

The overarching responsibility of any school team is to engage solution-finding strategies to solve identified problems and plan and implement educational and related support services that positively impact one or more students. The most effective problem-solving teams are ones comprised of individuals with diverse backgrounds, roles, and expertise that bring together divergent skills and perspectives. The authors have found that an optimally effective team includes among its members, those who:

1) have the needed expertise to solve the challenge (e.g., assistive technology specialist, behavior support specialist, English language learning specialist, math coach);

2) have direct experience with the student for whom the meeting has been convened (e.g., parent, classroom teacher, previous year's teacher, para-educator);

3) are affected by the decision (e.g., the person that the meeting is about, a paraeducator who works with the student and will help implement the solutions);

4) have an interest in and are invited by the person for whom the meeting has been convened (e.g., friend, siblings, classmate, grandparents).

Inclusive Education
Best Practice Checklist Assessment

Inclusive Education Best Practice #5:
Collaborative Planning and
Creative Problem Solving

<u>Directions</u>: Based upon your experience, please give each of the following 11 indicators a (zero to 4) rating in response to the question, "To what degree does this indicator occur in my school?"

0	1	2	3	4
Never	Rarely	Some of the time	Most of the time	Always

Rating (0 – 4)	Indicator of Collaborative Planning and Creative Problem Solving
☐	1. General and special education teachers *regularly collaborate* with one another and others (e.g., teachers of students identified as talented and gifted, English language learning specialists, related service providers, paraeducators, families) to plan, instruct, and evaluate the performance of students with and without disabilities.
☐	2. Related service personnel (e.g., speech/language therapists, physical therapists, psychologists, counselors, social workers) *regularly communicate* with general educators and other school personnel to *share information* about individual student strengths, needs, and services.
☐	3. Among the school's teams is a *general education creative problem-solving team* (e.g., Student Study Team, Student Success Team, MTSS/RtI team), which *meets regularly to assist classroom teachers in addressing individual student challenges* (e.g., academic, social-emotional/interpersonal, communication) and avoid unnecessary referrals for special education eligibility.

Rating (0 – 4)	Indicator of Collaborative Planning and Creative Problem Solving

4. The *assistance* provided by the school's general education problem-solving team is of high quality and *results in useful and usable solutions* and interventions to identified problems.

5. The *membership* of school problem-solving teams includes *individuals with the needed expertise* to solve the challenge (e.g., assistive technology specialist, behavior interventionist, English language learning specialist, math coach).

6. The *membership* of school problem-solving teams includes individuals with *direct experience* (e.g., parent, classroom teacher, previous year's teacher, paraeducator) with the student for whom the meeting has been convened.

7. The *membership* of school problem-solving teams includes the *individual(s) affected by the decision* (e.g., the person for whom the meeting has been convened, a paraeducator who works directly with the focus student and who will help implement the solution).

8. The *membership* of school problem-solving teams includes *individuals who have an interest in and are invited* by the individual for whom the meeting has been convened (e.g., siblings, classmates, grandparents).

9. Adequate *planning time* is provided for general and special educators, and other team members (e.g., psychologists, social workers, counselors) to collaborate.

10. General and special educators and problem-solving team members have received *training in collaborative teaming and creative problem-solving processes.*

Rating
(0 – 4)

Indicator of Collaborative Planning
and Creative Problem Solving

☐	11. Team members know and use a variety of *creative problem-solving strategies* (e.g., brainstorming, seeking additional information through questioning, meta-cognition, asking for the underlying rationale for a proposed solution or proposal, asking for critical feedback) to address issues.

Total Score (out of 44 maximum): _____

Mean Score (Total Score/11): _____

Range of Scores: _____ (low) to _____ (high)

Inclusive Education Best Practice #6:
Co-Teaching

6

Co-teaching may be defined as two or more people sharing responsibility for teaching all of the students assigned to a classroom (Villa, Thousand, & Nevin, 2013). Features of effective co-teaching include the distribution of responsibility among the co-teachers for planning, instructing, and evaluating the performance of their assigned students in mixed-ability classrooms. A common co-teaching partnership is between a general educator (a master of content) and a special educator (a master of access). Although this is the prevalent configuration, co-teaching teams may include reading specialists, math coaches, speech and language pathologists, teacher librarians, media specialists, English language learning specialists, therapists, paraeducators, and students themselves.

Co-teaching has been found to be effective in supporting students with a variety of needs in general education. Emerging research suggests that co-teaching allows for differentiation of instruction and curriculum access for all students. Namely, co-teaching increases the teacher-student ratio, provides students with access to the diverse and specialized knowledge and instructional approaches of their co-teachers, and enables co-teachers to more readily use research-proven teaching strategies (e.g., cooperative group learning). Co-teaching has been found to increase overall student achievement, decrease discipline referrals, and result in happier teachers who feel less isolated (Schwab Learning, 2003; Villa, Thousand, Nevin, 2013). Further, students with and without disabilities report having positive experiences in co-taught classrooms (Wilson & Michaels, 2006).

In successful co-teaching partnerships, where co-teachers move in and out of four co-teaching approaches based upon student and curriculum demands, students view both co-teachers as knowledgeable and credible. The four co-teaching approaches — supportive, parallel, complementary, and team — are defined and described in Table 2 (Villa et al., 2013).

Table 2.
Four Co-Teaching Approaches

Supportive co-teaching is when one teacher takes the lead instructional role while the other teacher(s) rotate among students and provide support. For example, the supportive co-teacher watches and listens as students work, stepping in to provide assistance as needed, while the lead teacher continues to direct the overall lesson.

Parallel co-teaching is when two or more people work with different groups of students in different sections of the classroom. Station teaching and monitoring of cooperative groups or lab station monitoring are examples of this approach.

Complementary co-teaching is when a co-teacher enhances the instruction provided by the other co-teacher. For example, one co-teacher might paraphrase the other's statements, model note-taking skills or use of a graphic organizer, develop anchor charts, or provide additional examples or analogies.

Team co-teaching is when two or more people do what the traditional teacher has done alone — plan, teach, assess, and assume responsibility for all of the students in the class. They both deliver content and both employ strategies to facilitate access to the general education curriculum. This approach has the most equitable distribution of duties. For example, co-teacher A might explain step one of an experiment while co-teacher B models the step. They switch roles and co-teacher B explains step two of the procedure while co-teacher A models that step.

Inclusive Education
Best Practice Checklist Assessment

Inclusive Education Best Practice #6:
Co-Teaching

Directions: Based upon your experience, please give each of the following 14 indicators a (zero to 4) rating in response to the question, "To what degree does this indicator occur in my school?"

0	1	2	3	4
Never	Rarely	Some of the time	Most of the time	Always

Rating Indicator of Co-Teaching
(0 – 4)

1. There is *widespread use of co-teaching* (i.e., two or more people sharing instructional responsibility for all of the students assigned to them) at the school site.

2. Co-teachers *share responsibility* for planning, teaching, and assessing the progress of all the students they share in common.

3. Regardless of which co-teaching approach is used, *all co-teachers* work with all students assigned to a classroom.

4. Co-teaching is viewed as a vehicle to provide quality *differentiated instruction.*

5. Co-teaching is *not viewed as voluntary,* but as required to ensure student support and curriculum access.

6. In addition to virtual planning (e.g., e-mailing, sharing of materials via e-mail or Google docs), partners who co-teach (e.g., classroom teachers, ELL teachers, special educators, related service providers) meet and collaboratively *plan face-to-face at least weekly* for a minimum of 45 - 60 minutes.

Rating   **Indicator of Co-Teaching**
(0 – 4)

☐ 7. On average, *co-taught classrooms* have *no more than 25%* of the students in a class identified as *eligible for special education* services, unless it is reflective of the demographic of the total school population.

☐ 8. Co-taught classrooms are *comprised of a mix of students who represent the overall population of the school* (e.g., academic and social performance, primary language, gender) rather than primarily students who struggle to learn, or are considered at-risk or lower achieving.

☐ 9. Co-teaching partners or teams *regularly remain together* for more than one year.

☐ 10. When using *parallel* co-teaching (i.e., students taught in groups) the *vast majority of the time,* students work in *heterogeneous, mixed-ability groups*.

☐ 11. In *parallel* co-teaching, when students are *grouped homogenously,* groupings are *fluid and flexible* and based upon *analysis of student performance data* rather than eligibility for special education or other services.

☐ 12. In *parallel* co-teaching, when students are grouped homogenously, students are *not grouped based upon a particular label* (e.g., eligible for special education, English learner), but based upon the need for extension or a particular instructional intervention or strategy.

☐ 13. Co-teaching approaches are *regularly used at all three tiers* of MTSS/RtI[2] (i.e., core instruction, supplemental, and intensive).

☐ 14. Co-teachers use *all four* (i.e., supportive, parallel, complementary, team) co-teaching aproaches, rather than relying primarily on supportive or parallel approaches.

Total Score (out of 56 maximum):   _____

Mean Score (Total Score/14):   _____

Range of Scores: _____ (low) to   _____ (high)

Inclusive Education Best Practice #7:

Student-Centered Strength-Based Assessment

Accurate assessment of student learning requires students to have multiple means for expressing their understanding of the curriculum. Frameworks such as Multiple Intelligence theory (Gardner, 2011) and learning and thinking styles (Gregory & Chapman, 2013) assist educators to think about assessing students in various ways. For example, through his research, Gardner found a singular construct of intelligence to be too narrow. Instead, he identified multiple (currently 8) dimensions of intelligence: visual-spatial, musical-rhythmic, bodily-kinesthetic, interpersonal, intrapersonal, naturalistic, verbal-linguistic and logical-mathematical. Falvey, Blair, Dingle, and Franklin (2000) point out the benefits of this view of intelligence with regard to student assessment:

> The question that educators and psychologists often struggle with is: How smart is the student? Gardner suggested that this is the wrong question to ask. The question that needs to be addressed is: How is this student smart? This question presumes that all students are smart; they are just smart in different ways. (p. 194)

Additional examples of varied assessment strategies that allow students to communicate what they really know and have learned are authentic performance assessments, such as curriculum-based assessment, artifact collections, portfolios, demonstrations, as well as the use of learning contracts and technology. Students who use assistive technology and augmentative communication systems to communicate and access learning also rely upon these technological supports to show what they really know.

An example of a person-centered and family-friendly authentic assessment process is Making Action Plans (MAPs) (Villa, Thousand, & Nevin, 2010). MAPs is particularly useful for students with more extensive support needs, whose lives and needs may be so complex that it is not always clear which directions are the "correct" ones to take. The MAPs process begins by assembling a team that includes the student, family members, peers and friends, and anyone else the student and family wants in attendance, including school personnel. With the help of a neutral facilitator, the team addresses a sequence of questions that identify the team members' and student's understanding of the student's history, strengths and gifts, dreams, and fears in order to visualize a desired close or more distant future and prioritize actions to achieve that future. The actions can be translated into school-based activities such as IEP goals, transition goals, activities to discover a student's strengths and abilities, and the development of self-determination skills. Actions also can be translated into activities outside of school that can be supported by members of the student's other support circles—family members, friends, and members of groups with which the student affiliates (e.g., local recreation center, gym, YMCA/YWCA).

Inclusive Education
Best Practice Checklist Assessment

Inclusive Education Best Practice #7:
Student-Centered Strength-Based Assessment

<u>Directions</u>: Based upon your experience, please give each of the following 8 indicators a (zero to 4) rating in response to the question, "To what degree does this indicator occur in my school?"

0	1	2	3	4
Never	Rarely	Some of the time	Most of the time	Always

Rating (0 – 4)	Indicator of Student-Centered Strength-Based Assessment
☐	1. The school provides information to families regarding *dynamic, authentic assessment processes* (e.g., curriculum-based assessment, artifact collections, portfolios, demonstrations) as well traditional evaluation processes (e.g., standardized assessments such as statewide testing, report cards).
☐	2. IEP teams do not solely rely upon standardized assessment, but also *student-centered, strength-based and family-focused assessments* (e.g., Multiple Intelligences, MAPs, self-determination) to get to know a student's history, characteristics, strengths, fears, and dreams.
☐	3. *Family members' input* regarding their child's strengths as well as ideas for effective adaptations and accommodations are both *solicited and considered.*
☐	4. Students are provided opportunities to *learn about their strengths and talents,* the impact of their disability, and *strategies to advocate* for what they need to accommodate their disability.

Rating (0 – 4)	Indicator of Student-Centered Strength-Based Assessment
☐	5. Students who are non-native English speakers have the opportunity to be *assessed in their primary language* and have an interpreter, if needed.
☐	6. Assessment reports and the present level of performance statements on the IEP are *written in language* that describes a student's current *strengths* (skills, preferences, current performance) rather than what the student does not yet know or do.
☐	7. IEP team members *use student's strengths, talents, and interests,* as well as other assessment data (achievement data, family member input), to determine *supports and services,* and plan for a student's desired future.
☐	8. *Students are taught about the IEP process* and supported and *coached to have a voice in determining their goals,* supports, and services by leading all or part of their IEP planning meeting.

Total Score (out of 32 maximum): _____

Mean Score (Total Score/8): _____

Range of Scores: _____ (low) to _____ (high)

Inclusive Education Best Practice #8:

Strategies for Facilitating Access to the General Education Curriculum

More than a decade ago Congress noted that, "nearly 30 years of research and experience has demonstrated that outcomes for students with disabilities can be made more effective by having high expectations for such children and ensuring their access to the general education curriculum to the maximum extent possible" (IDEIA, 2004). As general education classrooms become more inclusive, educators need to develop strategies for providing involvement and progress in the general education curriculum. There need to be collaborative opportunities to define and develop a vision in public education where all students, including students with disabilities, actively engage in learning and progress in the general curriculum.

Access to the general education curriculum is not exclusively a special education concern; it is dependent upon factors associated with the curriculum as well as instructional and assessment practices. The key to ensuring that a student with a disability can meaningfully participate in the general education curriculum is the creative thinking of the members of the student's IEP team. A team always has options for a student to contribute to and participate in the general education classroom (Giangreco, Cloninger, & Iverson, 2011; Giangreco, Dymond, & Shogren, 2016; Ohtake,

2003). Table 3 (on page 63) summarizes four participation options described by Giangreco and colleagues (2011, 2016). Key to determining which participation option to expect of a student and avoiding underestimating a student's ability is to presume competence and first consider having a student do the same thing as everyone else before proceeding down the list of options.

Table 3.
Four Participation Options

Little or No Accommodations Needed is when a student can do the same as everyone else or basically the same with minor modifications or supports typically available in a classroom (e.g., classmate support, preferential seating/positioning, extended time, reduced amount).

Multi-Level Curriculum and Instruction is when all students are involved in a lesson in the same curriculum area, but are pursuing varying objectives at multiple levels. For example, students applying math computation skills at varying levels—some with complex word problems, others with one-digit subtraction problems, and yet others with materials that illustrate counting with one-to-one correspondence.

Curriculum Overlapping involves students working on the same lesson, but pursuing objectives from different curricular areas. For example, Bob, a teenager with significant disabilities, was working in a cooperative group in science class, using the lap tray attached to his wheelchair as the team's workspace. Bob was expected to identify fewer body parts than the other group members. This opportunity was also taken to address other IEP objectives from the curriculum areas of communication and socialization. One communication objective (object discrimination) was simple for Bob's lab partners to facilitate throughout a dissection activity. Another motor objective (range of motion) was achieved by students using hand-under-hand assistance so Bob could pass the dissection instruments and engage in some of the dissection. Before moving to curriculum overlapping as a participation option, first explore how the use of universal design for learning principles might provide all students the communication and access supports to participate in instruction and assessment in the general education curriculum.

Alternative Activities may be needed in a student's schedule to allow for management needs (e.g., catheterization in the nurse's office requiring privacy) or when a general education activity cannot be adapted (e.g., mandatory statewide high stakes paper and pencil test). Caution is advised when deciding to remove a student from general education settings.

Inclusive Education
Best Practice Checklist Assessment

Inclusive Education Best Practice #8:
Strategies for Facilitating Access to the General Education Curriculum

Directions: Based upon your experience, please give each of the following 7 indicators a (zero to 4) rating in response to the question, "To what degree does this indicator occur in my school?"

0	1	2	3	4
Never	Rarely	Some of the time	Most of the time	Always

Rating (0 – 4) **Indicator of Use of Strategies for Facilitating Access to the General Education Curriculum**

1. School personnel view *effective instruction in general education* classroom settings as the foundation upon which to build and provide inclusive services.

2. In each child's Individual Education Program (IEP) planning meeting/conference, the *first placement option* considered is the *general education classroom* environment with the use of supplemental supports, aids, and services. There is a *presumption of placement* in the general education setting, with needed special education services, supplementary aids and services, and related services required for the student to be involved with and progress in the general education curriculum.

3. Each member of a student's *IEP planning team* has a documented *responsibility* to the student and the student's success in *inclusive environments*.

Rating (0 – 4)	Indicator of Use of Strategies for Facilitating Access to the General Education Curriculum
☐	4. General education teachers have specific knowledge regarding the *strengths* and needs of students with and without IEPs, and they assist and support *all students* in reaching their *potential*.
☐	5. A student's *special education classification* or eligibility category (e.g., intellectual disability, multiple disabilities, deaf-blindness, autism) *does* NOT determine or *limit* the *expectations* that school personnel have for that student.
☐	6. The school provides school staff regular, high quality professional development on how to *support students* with *varying abilities* to *access, interact with,* and *progress in* the general education curriculum.
☐	7. IEP teams *presume competence* of all students and consider various *participation options* in general education, *first considering* having a student *do the same thing* as everyone else before considering the other options identified in Table 3.

Total Score (out of 28 maximum):   _____

Mean Score (Total Score/7):   _____

Range of Scores: _____ (low) to   _____ (high)

Inclusive Education Best Practice #9:
Differentiation of Instruction

D ifferentiation of instruction — or differentiated instruction — is both a *frame of mind* as well as a *teaching process.* Willis & Mann (2000) emphasize differentiation of instruction as a *teaching philosophy* based upon the premise that teachers should adapt instruction to student differences because *one size does not fit all.* According to Hall, Strangman, and Meyer (2011), researchers at the National Center on Accessing the General Curriculum, differentiation of instruction is also an *instructional process* that recognizes and *acknowledges the differences* among students' background knowledge, readiness, language, culture, and learning preferences and interests, and then reacts *responsively and positively* to these natural differences.

Differentiated instruction is a process for teaching students who vary in how they learn in the same classroom. It is way for teachers to proactively plan for and respond to *individual differences* via a process of adapting and modifying materials, learning goals, instructional methods and learning activities, and what students are required to do and produce in a classroom (Universal Design for Learning, 2013). Stated otherwise, differentiated instruction requires teachers to provide students with multiple means of *representation* (content differentiation), multiple means of *engagement* (process differentiation) and multiple means of *expression* (product differentiation). To do this requires attention and differentiation at what has come to be known as the four instructional *access design points* (i.e., facts about the students, content, product, process) described in Table 4.

Table 4.
The Four Access Design Points for Differentiating Instruction

Access Design Point #1: Gather Facts About the Students
Educators who differentiate must first gather facts about the differences in students' background knowledge, readiness, language, culture, and learning preferences and interests.

Access Design Point #2: Content Demands
Given this information about students, educators then differentiate content. Content is multidimensional because it involves not only what is to be taught and differentiated for students, but variations in learning objectives and levels of knowledge and proficiency students need to demonstrate, as well as variations in the materials to be used.

Access Design Point #3: Product Demands
This product access design point concerns how students show what they know and have learned and how their products are evaluated. Information gathered about student learning preference can be used to enable students to best show what they have learned. Standardized assessments are augmented with authentic assessment processes (e.g., portfolios, curriculum-based assessment, direct observation of performance).

Access Design Point #4: Process Demands
This process design point requires teachers to consider how best to help students make sense of what they are to learn. Teachers use various lesson formats and arrangements (e.g., discovery learning, cooperative group learning, direct instruction), technology, and evidence-based instructional practices and scaffolds to provide access for every student.

In summary, the intent of differentiating instruction is to maximize each student's growth and individual success by meeting each student where he or she is in the curriculum, and assisting each student to learn via his or her unique learning processes. Differentiated instruction is a way to *shake things up in the classroom,* changing how teachers teach so that all students have access to powerful and effective learning. Notably, differentiation of instruction can best and most easily occur for every child when general educators and specialists (special educators) rethink how to deliver their expertise and services. Differentiation most easily and naturally occurs when educators collaborate in planning and instruction to not only accommodate the learning differences of students with IEPs, English learners, students considered gifted and talented, and students otherwise considered at-risk (e.g., impacted by homelessness), but to *accommodate the learning differences experienced by all students through instructional delivery arrangements such as co-teaching* rather than pullout services.

Inclusive Education
Best Practice Checklist Assessment

Inclusive Education Best Practice #9:
Differentiation of Instruction

Directions: Based upon your experience, please give each of the
following 10 indicators a (zero to 4) rating in response to the question, "To what degree does this indicator occur in my school?"

0	1	2	3	4
Never	Rarely	Some of the time	Most of the time	Always

Rating (0 – 4) **Indicator of Differentiation of Instruction**

1. Instructional personnel understand that they have a
responsibility to proactively *adapt instruction* to
accommodate student differences.

2. Instructional personnel have had explicit and extensive *training* in and understand what constitutes
differentiated instruction.

3. Instructional personnel *gather data (facts) about students* from varying multiple sources (e.g., record review,
interview, survey, interest inventories, observation,
learning styles inventory, formative and summative
assessment) in order to *differentiate instruction in*
response to their students' varying background knowledge, interests, strengths, culture, language, learning
preferences, and means of communication (e.g., alternative and augmentative communication).

4. Within each unit of study, *content and materials differentiation* routinely occurs, with students being
offered *multiple options for taking in information*
(e.g., texts with varying readability levels, text-to-

Rating
(0 – 4)

Indicator of Differentiation of Instruction

speech/text reader software and apps, auditory and visual input, word walls, graphic organizers, layered curricula, curriculum compacting).

5. Within each unit of study, *product and assessment differentiation* routinely occurs, with students being offered *multiple ways to express what they have learned* (e.g., written products, PowerPoint products, podcasts, summary of interviews, oral presentation) and being graded in a variety of ways (e.g., bench-mark assessments, contracts, IEP goal attainment, portfolios).

6. Within each unit of study, *process differentiation* routinely occurs to help students make sense of the ideas, concepts, procedures, and principles being taught through the use of *multiple instructional formats* (e.g., adapted lectures, hands-on, computer and web-based, stations and centers, simulation, role play, thematic unit or lesson, community referenced, service learning, self directed, culturally responsive techniques).

7. Within each unit of study, *process differentiation* routinely occurs to help students make sense of the ideas, concepts, procedures, and principles being taught through the use of *multiple instructional arrangements* (e.g., cooperative learning structures, same or cross-age peer tutors, teacher directed small groups, independent study, large group instruction).

8. Within each unit of study, *process differentiation* routinely occurs to help students make sense of the ideas, concepts, procedures, and principles being taught through the use of *multiple instructional strategies* (e.g., multiple intelligence theory, integration of the arts, use of taxonomies, research-based strategies).

Rating   Indicator of Differentiation of Instruction
(0 – 4)

☐ 9. Within each unit of study, *process differentiation* routinely occurs to help students make sense of the ideas, concepts, procedures, and principles being taught through *alterations of the physical environment* (e.g., room arrangement, accessibility of materials, preferential seating) *and/or social environment* (e.g., teaching of social norms, behavior contracts, Positive Behavior Supports).

☐ 10. Instructional personnel collaborate to *share* differentiated *lessons and unit plans.*

Total Score (out of 40 maximum): _____

Mean Score (Total Score/10): _____

Range of Scores: _____ **(low) to** _____ **(high)**

Inclusive Education
Best Practice #10:
Student Empowerment And Natural Peer Supports

"The future world suggests a new collaborative role for teachers and students in which students accept an active senior partnership role in the learning enterprise." — (Benjamin, 1989, p. 9)

Agreeing with Benjamin's 1989 observation, Villa, Thousand, and Nevin (2010) argue that the future is now — that engaging students in collaborative roles in teaching and decision making is essential and beneficial, because it:

1. facilitates 21st century goals of education,

2. represents democratic schooling,

3. increases student self-determination,

4. increases student academic and social competence,

5. facilitates other school reform efforts, and

6. represents an untapped instructional resource in an era of limited fiscal and human resources.

People who work in inclusive schools have discovered the importance of practicing what they preach about collaboration and distributed leadership by sharing their instructional and decision-making power with students in a climate of mutual respect. Among the limitless student collaboration roles that benefit students and educators alike are: 1) students as instructors in cooperative group learning, partner learning, and adult-student co-teaching teams; 2) students sitting on planning teams (e.g., IEP teams, transition planning teams, teams to determine accommodations and modifications) for themselves and classmates; and 3) students sharing decision-making responsibility by serving on decision-making bodies such as school boards and hiring, curriculum, and discipline committees.

To maximize student learning and to promote individual independence and autonomy, educators must design instruction that allots significant control to students and is carried out in inclusive educational environments with *natural supports* whenever possible. Rogan, Hagner, and Murphy (1993) simply and clearly define natural supports as any "assistance, relationships, or interactions [voluntarily given] that allow a person to secure, maintain, and advance" in school and work settings (p. 275). *Natural peer supports* are such supports provided by classmates and schoolmates. Taking and sharing one's notes with a student who has difficulty writing is an example of a natural peer support. It should be emphasized that caring for and sharing responsibility for one another is a major characteristic of inclusive schools and communities. Thus, natural peer supports are a process and an outcome that should be encouraged and sustained.

Inclusive Education
Best Practice Checklist Assessment

Inclusive Education Best Practice #10:
Student Empowerment and Natural Peer Supports

Directions: Based upon your experience, please give each of the following 10 indicators a (zero to 4) rating in response to the question, "To what degree does this indicator occur in my school?"

0	1	2	3	4
Never	Rarely	Some of the time	Most of the time	Always

Rating (0 – 4)	Indicator of Student Empowerment and Natural Peer Supports
	1. The school's *philosophy and mission statement* clearly value and encourage student *self-determination and empowerment* in instruction and decision making.
	2. School staff deliberately attend to and promote *positive social interactions* among students.
	3. When needed, students' IEPs include goals that help develop *self-advocacy, self-determination,* and *independence skills.*
	4. Inside and outside of the classroom, general educators and support personnel structure *natural peer supports* for students with and without disabilities who need support before considering and providing support from adults.
	5. Students are encouraged to *advocate for themselves* and others and receive support and training to do so by attending and *actively participating in meetings* important to themselves and their peers (e.g., IEP meetings, transition planning meetings, Section 504

Rating (0 – 4)	Indicator of Student Empowerment and Natural Peer Supports

planning meetings and other meetings to determine accommodations and modifications).

☐ 6. Students are deliberately and *actively engaged as decision makers* in classroom and school affairs (e.g., determination of classroom rules and consequences, school governance and decision-making committees, parent-teacher-student conferences).

☐ 7. Students are explicitly taught the skills necessary to work in *cooperative learning groups* and frequently work in cooperative learning groups where they engage in shared learning and are interdependent upon and accountable for one another.

☐ 8. Students are explicitly taught the skills necessary to engage in *same-age and cross-age peer tutoring* arrangements, in which students with and without disabilities have opportunities to tutor other learners in their class and school. Peer tutoring arrangements are widely used.

☐ 9. Students receive training and opportunities to learn how to use *alternative and augmentative communication (AAC) systems* needed to communicate with classmates who use these devices and systems.

☐ 10. Students are recruited, trained, and serve as *co-teachers* alongside their adult teachers in the school.

Total Score (out of 40 maximum): _____

Mean Score (Total Score/10): _____

Range of Scores: _____ (low) to _____ (high)

Inclusive Education
Best Practice #11:

Multi-Tiered System of Supports (MTSS)/
Response to Instruction and Intervention (RtI²)

The notion of a *Multi-Tiered System of Supports (MTSS)* was first introduced in the 2004 reauthorization of the Individuals with Disabilities Education Act (IDEA) as an instructional system for preventing unnecessary special education referral by providing research-based instruction in general education and swift and targeted interventions to accelerate learning among struggling students. Originally termed *Response to Intervention (RtI)*, this system is conceptualized as a three-tiered "pyramid" approach, with Tier 1 being high quality evidence-based core instruction in general education, with frequent student progress monitoring. Tier 2 represents the supplemental targeted and strategic interventions, generally delivered in small groups to students not making adequate progress on expected curriculum benchmarks. Tier 3 represents the intensive (more frequent and individualized) interventions for students whose response to intervention at Tiers 1 and 2 is deemed inadequate (Villa & Thousand, 2011). In California, RtI has been renamed *Response to Intervention and Instruction or RtI²*, to emphasize the importance of a foundation of high quality instruction in general education.

The Multitiered System of Supports or MTSS language has emerged recently as an umbrella concept and label for a comprehensive system of support, which not only strives to prevent unnecessary referrals for special education, but to provide a comprehensive school-wide and district-wide system of "high-quality first instruction, supports, and interventions in academics and behavior for all students, regardless of whether they are struggling or have advanced learning needs" (California Services for Technical Assistance and Training, 2015, p. 2). MTSS provides an overarching organizing structure not only for RtI/RtI^2 processes, but also for *Schoolwide Positive Behavior Support (SWPBS)* systems supporting social-emotional-behavioral health and growth, and *Universal Design for Learning (UDL)* practices of automatically differentiating instructional content (e.g., curriculum, materials, learning goals), products (e.g., assessments and performance expectations), and processes (e.g., moment-to-moment interaction of students with content and with one another) based upon the natural learning differences of students in any classroom (Thousand, Villa, and Nevin, 2015).

Inclusive Education
Best Practice Checklist Assessment

Inclusive Education Best Practice #11:
Multi-Tiered System of Supports (MTSS)/
Response to Instruction and Intervention (RtI²)

Directions: Based upon your experience, please give each of the following 12 indicators a (zero to 4) rating in response to the question, "To what degree does this indicator occur in my school?"

0	1	2	3	4
Never	Rarely	Some of the time	Most of the time	Always

Rating (0 – 4)	Indicator of Multi-Tiered System of Supports (MTSS)/ Response to Instruction and Intervention (RtI²)
☐	1. District and school *goals* for students are *prevention of school failure* and *prevention of unnecessary referral* for assessment for *special education* eligibility.
☐	2. The building *administrator explicitly supports* in word and actions and regularly *links MTSS/RtI² efforts to overarching goals for all* children and goals of preventing school failure and unnecessary referral for special education.
☐	3. Educators provide *high quality, research-based instruction* in general education classrooms for all students
☐	4. Teachers use *fluid and flexible grouping* of students for instruction, remediation, and enrichment.
☐	5. A *well-articulated and well-understood* Multi-Tiered System of Supports (MTSS)/Response to Instruction and Intervention (RtI²) system is in place.
☐	6. The MTSS/RtI² system uses regular, periodic (e.g., three times per year) screening of the entire school

Rating (0 – 4)	Indicator of Multi-Tiered System of Supports (MTSS)/ Response to Instruction and Intervention (RtI²)

population to determine and deliver early intervention for any student.

☐ 7. The MTSS/RtI² system *brings services to students without* having to *label* the child (e.g., as special education eligible) or make a child eligible for special education.

☐ 8. The MTSS/RtI² system provides *research-based interventions at increasing levels of intensity* (e.g., at Tier 2 and Tier 3) for students who do not make adequate, expected progress before considering referral for assessment for special education.

☐ 9. The MTSS/RtI² system provides *continuous progress monitoring during interventions.*

☐ 10. A schoolwide *integrated data system* is used to ensure *student progress data are accurate, available, and used to make instructional decisions.*

☐ 11. The MTSS/RtI² system *closely monitors group composition* to assure that membership does not remain static and result in de facto tracking.

☐ 12. The school and district have a *routine for program evaluation and continuous improvement* of the MTSS/RtI² system.

Total Score (out of 48 maximum): _____

Mean Score (Total Score/12): _____

Range of Scores: _____ **(low) to** _____ **(high)**

Inclusive Education Best Practice #12:
Positive Behavioral Supports (PBS)

Individuals who experience and exhibit behaviors that are considered challenging in a school environment are at risk of many negative outcomes: removal from the school or general education classroom and placement in a more restrictive, segregated setting, loss of interpersonal relationships with peers, and negative interventions (e.g., use of psychotropic drugs, punishment responses). *Positive Behavior Support (PBS)* is an alternative to responding with restrictive intervention responses and segregated placement.

The primary purpose of PBS is to minimize and prevent behaviors that interfere with learning and interacting with others through the use of positive behavioral approaches (O'Neill & Jameson, 2016). These approaches start with setting schoolwide and individual student behavioral expectations, teaching expectations, and recognizing and rewarding norm-following behaviors. They are further individualized for students with more frequent or intensive disruptive behaviors via direct instruction of impulse control, problem solving, and social skills; contracts, daily check-in and check-out systems with daily progress reports; and frequent and salient praise and positive consequences for achieving goals. A second and equally important purpose of PBS is to enhance the quality of life for students who experience and exhibit challenging behaviors by pursuing a lifestyle change, if you will, in addition to pursuing academic goals.

Schoolwide PBS (SWPBS) is the behavioral side of Inclusive Education Best Practice #11: Multi-Tiered System of Supports (MTSS)/Response to Instruction and Intervention (RtI²). Implementing a Schoolwide PBS system requires a shift to inclusive values and practices toward students perceived as behaviorally challenging. It requires the construction of a culture of competence; namely, that it is the school community's responsibility to define, teach, monitor, and reward rule-following behavior as well as academic progress. It requires working with rather than sending away students whose behavior is unsettling. It requires the examination of why challenging behavior occurs, what the function of the behavior is for the student, what need the behavior is meeting or not meeting. It requires data collection to determine the impact of not just academic, but behavioral interventions.

Inclusive Education
Best Practice Checklist Assessment

Inclusive Education Best Practice #12:
Positive Behavioral Supports

Directions: Based upon your experience, please give each of the
following 13 indicators a (zero to 4) rating in response to the question, "To what degree does this indicator occur in my school?"

0	1	2	3	4
Never	Rarely	Some of the time	Most of the time	Always

Rating   Indicator of Positive Behavioral Supports
(0 – 4)

1. School personnel view it as everyone's responsibility to
   define, teach, monitor, and reward rule-following
   behavior as well as academic progress (these features
   comprise a Culture of Competence).

2. Instructional and administrative personnel direct a
   system of accountability, to ensure *consistent and
   schoolwide application* of the school's *Positive Behavior Support* approach and system.

3. A *well-articulated Schoolwide PBS (SWPBS)* system is
   part of the school's Multi-Tiered System of Supports
   (MTSS)/Response to Instruction and Intervention
   (RtI^2) approach to supporting academic and behav-
   ioral/social learning.

4. Designated school personnel (e.g., a SWPBS core team,
   grade level teams) are provided time to collaborate,
   develop, and *monitor the SWPBS* system.

5. Teachers and other school staff receive *quality training*
   in *positive behavioral support* approaches.

Rating **Indicator of Positive Behavioral Supports**
(0 – 4)

---

6. School staff *deliberately and routinely use positive behavioral supports* to promote a sense of *community and safety* for all students.

7. Teachers and other school personnel *understand and believe* that *behavior* is often a form of communication, frequently about unmet needs.

8. When a student shows recurring or intensified disruptive behavior, the *typical response is a team approach* to determine the *function of the behavior* in order to *develop comprehensive interventions and supports* rather than seeking special education eligibility or placing the student in a more restrictive setting outside of the school or the general education classroom.

9. The team developing a behavior intervention plan for a student has *comprehensive and diverse membership* (e.g., general and special educators, related service personnel including personnel with positive behavior support expertise, an administrator), including the student.

10. The school's *first step* in developing a positive behavior support plan for a student is to *collect data* about the student's *strengths and other characteristics* as well as about the context(s) in which the troubling behavior occurs (i.e., antecedents and consequences).

11. The *next step* in developing a positive behavior support plan for a student is to identify possible *unmet needs* of the student (e.g., lack of academic success) that might be driving behavior. Every effort is made to gain the student's perspective and experience of the situation.

Rating   **Indicator of Positive Behavioral Supports**
(0 – 4)

___

☐ 12. A safe and ethical *crisis and emergency response intervention plan* has been developed to support students whose behaviors may escalate and pose a danger to themselves or others.

☐ 13. Staff is adequately *trained* to handle *medical/ behavioral emergencies* in the classrooms.

Total Score (out of 52 maximum):   _____

Mean Score (Total Score/13):   _____

Range of Scores: _____ (low) to   _____ (high)

Inclusive Education Best Practice #13:

Integrated Delivery of Related Services

Related services can be defined as any developmental, corrective, or other supportive services required so that students with disabilities benefit from their educational program, where *benefit* is defined as progress toward and achievement of Individual Education Program goals and participation and progress in the general education curriculum. Related service personnel can provide students with disabilities access to an appropriate education and facilitate students' pursuit of important learning outcomes by applying specific skills associated with their respective disciplines through effective collaboration with others (Rainforth & York-Barr, 1997).

Increasingly, students with complex disabilities and more extensive support needs are being educated in general education classroom settings. With this increase comes a corresponding increase in the need for various related services (e.g., speech and language services, occupational and physical therapy, counseling and other psychological services, therapeutic recreation, assistive technology) in schools and general education classrooms. A best practice in delivering related service support in inclusive settings is known as *role release*, the process whereby a specialist's knowledge and skills are imparted through modeling, consultation, collaborative planning and co-teaching to members of a student's IEP team, including the student's teachers, peers, and family members.

Regular and ongoing communication among members of a student's IEP team is essential to ensuring that related services and general and special education services are delivered in a way that avoids undesirable or unnecessary gaps, overlaps, and contradictions among IEP and other learning goals, services, and activities (Giangreco, 2016; Giangreco, Prelock, Reid, Dennis, & Edelman, 2000). Stated otherwise, communication is essential to ensure that individually-determined student supports are delivered in an *integrated* fashion that 1) effectively achieves specified outcomes, 2) uses resources in a responsible manner, 3) is status enhancing or status neutral for the student, and 4) is only as specialized as necessary—enough but not too much (Giangreco, 1996; 2016).

Determining whether or not a related service is needed for a student with an IEP is a complex and nuanced professional team decision. Giangreco (2016) describes a decision-making process for determining if a related service is needed for a student. He argues that to be worthy of inclusion as a service in an IEP, the IEP team must agree that the service is *both relevant* and *necessary* and answer "yes" to both of two questions. Question #1 assesses whether or not the service is relevant by asking, "If the student does not receive the proposed related service, is there reason to believe that s/he would not experience educational benefit?" Clearly Question #1 is likely to be answered "yes" for any number of potential related services—music therapy, surfing therapy, art therapy, physical and occupational therapy, and dozens of others that come up in the authors' experience as San Diego residents! If the team answers "yes," the related service is relevant. If the answer is "no," the case is closed; the proposed service is NOT an IEP-appropriate service. Question #2 assesses the *necessary* question. This is the tougher question to answer. It asks, "If the student does not receive the proposed related service, is there reason to believe that s/he would not have access to a free appropriate public education [which is required by law]?" This often becomes a judgment call on the part of the team members, as the "reason to believe" is very much driven by professional judgment. The bottom line: related services are important, most often relevant, but not always necessary. For more on the decision-making sub-questions and examples, see Giangreco (2016).

Inclusive Education
Best Practice Checklist Assessment

Inclusive Education Best Practice #13:
Integrated Delivery of Related Services

<u>Directions</u>: Based upon your experience, please give each of the following 5 indicators a (zero to 4) rating in response to the question, "To what degree does this indicator occur in my school?"

0	1	2	3	4
Never	Rarely	Some of the time	Most of the time	Always

Rating (0 – 4)	Indicator of Integrated Delivery of Related Services
☐	1. Related service personnel (e.g., speech and language pathologists, occupational and physical therapists, psychologists, social workers, assistive technology consultants, counselors) *communicate* with one another and other school personnel and family members to *share information* about student's strengths and needs and to *plan for services.*
☐	2. School staff *work closely* with related service personnel to *integrate* related services into the school day and week in *inclusive* general education settings.
☐	3. The school's *leadership* (principal) *expects and supports collaboration* among general educators, special educators, and related service personnel to ensure integrated delivery of related services in inclusive classroom and school environments.
☐	4. Related service personnel practice *role release*—the sharing of knowledge and skills through modeling, consultation, collaborative planning and co-teaching with educators, parents, paraeducators, and students—

Rating (0 – 4)	Indicator of Integrated Delivery of Related Services
	to address related service goals within inclusive classroom and school environments.
☐	5. When the IEP team deems a related service to be both *relevant* and *necessary*, the team includes the service in the IEP.

Total Score (out of 20 maximum): _____

Mean Score (Total Score/5): _____

Range of Scores: _____ (low) to _____ (high)

Inclusive Education Best Practice #14:
Transition Planning

School is full of transitions—transitions from preschool, elementary school, middle school, and high school, and to post-secondary life, with various learning, career, and living options. Students with disabilities, just like students without disabilities, experience these transitions. Without careful planning by students' IEP teams, these transitions can lead to fewer opportunities for participation in age-appropriate general education and integrated community activities for individuals with disabilities. Transition planning involves a number of stakeholders, including general and special educators, the student, family members, related services personnel who provide services, and anyone else important in the student's life, such as friends. Transition planning provides students and their families the opportunity to set goals for the next school setting and make connections with the teachers and service providers in the next school setting. To best facilitate transitions, anticipate problems, and provide interventions, the planning process should involve appropriate persons from the present and the future environments and occur well in advance of the actual transition. Clearly, the planning process needs to actively and meaningfully put students with disabilities in the director's chair and maximize the extent to which the process is student-directed and self-regulated.

The transition from high school to adult life often is the most exciting and anticipated, as well as most anxiety provoking for students and their families. For students with disabilities, the federal mandate that guarantees them a free and appropriate education in the least restrictive environment expires upon exit from the public school system with graduation or at some time around age 22. Careful transition planning is needed to ensure that post-secondary life resembles that which the student, family, and those who care about the student desire for his or her life. Fortunately, the federal Individuals with Disabilities Education Improvement Act (IDEIA) requires that students with disabilities receive transition services and that each student's Individual Education Program (IEP) include a transition component — Individual Transition Plan (ITP) — beginning no later than age 16. The 2004 reauthorization of IDEA clearly defines what transition services should accomplish and holds schools accountable for these accomplishments. Namely, the law requires

> ... a coordinated set of activities ... focused
> on improving the academic and functional
> achievement... to facilitate the child's movement
> from school to post-school activities, including
> post-secondary education, vocational education,
> integrated employment, continuing and adult
> education, adult services, independent living...
> (20 U.S.C. § 1401 sec. 602 [35])

Post-secondary transition planning involves several steps: (1) identifying a student's strengths, preferences, dreams, needs and present levels of performance through a variety of formal and informal assessments; (2) developing post-secondary goals and associated annual IEP goals to prepare the student to achieve those goals, and (3) identifying services that will help the student, while still in school, to achieve the post-secondary goals. Central, and required by law, is the student's active participation in this ITP planning process. *Person-centered* or *person-driven planning* is a transition planning approach that specifically focuses on future outcomes and the quality of life and dreams of a student, and elicits the student's voice and the voices of those who care most about the student in this future planning. Making Action Plans (Villa, Thousand, and Nevin, 2010) is an example of a person-centered planning process that engages a wide circle of people in thinking about a person's history, attributes and gifts, and that person's and participant's dreams and fears for the future in order to create a plan that moves toward the dreams and avoids the fears. Person-centered planning processes play an important role in preparing for the future lives and goals of students with disabilities, and should be a part of any transition planning process.

Inclusive Education
Best Practice Checklist Assessment

Inclusive Education Best Practice #14:
Transition Planning

Directions: Based upon your experience, please give each of the following 6 indicators a (zero to 4) rating in response to the question, "To what degree does this indicator occur in my school?"

0	1	2	3	4
Never	Rarely	Some of the time	Most of the time	Always

Rating (0 – 4)   **Indicator of Transition Planning**

☐   1. A *well-defined planning process to facilitate successful transition* of students with disabilities from grade to grade, school to school, and from secondary school to post-secondary life is used. This process is not limited to the mandatory Individual Transition Plan required of students with IEPs by age 16.

☐   2. A *person-centered, person-driven transition planning process is used* to facilitate students with disabilities thinking about their dreams for the near and distant future, and plan for transitions (grade to grade, school to school, secondary school to post-secondary life).

☐   3. Students with disabilities are *provided instruction and supports to actively* and meaningfully *plan their futures* and maximize the extent to which the process is student-directed and self-regulated.

☐   4. The *transition planning process* for a student with disabilities is *collaborative*, with a student's general and special educators, family members, involved related services personnel, the student, and anyone important in the student's life (such as friends) actively

**Rating
(0 – 4)**   **Indicator of Transition Planning**

sought out, invited, and involved in the process. [Note: For Individual Transition Plans, required by age 16, representatives from adult service organizations and agencies (e.g., post-secondary education, vocational education, integrated employment, continuing and adult education, adult services, independent living) are invited.]

☐ 5. The transition planning process *identifies*, through the variety of formal and informal assessments, a student's *strengths, preferences, dreams, needs,* and present levels of performance.

☐ 6. Transition planning emphasizes the continuation or *expansion over time* of *inclusive education opportunities* across grade levels, schools, and post-secondary life for students.

Total Score (out of 24 maximum): _____

Mean Score (Total Score/6): _____

Range of Scores: _____ (low) to _____ (high)

Inclusive Education Best Practice #15:
Site-Based Continuous Planning for Sustainability

Inclusive education best practices are easily understood and implemented in school communities that have restructured or are on the journey of restructuring to meet the needs of an increasingly diverse student population. General education organizational best practices (e.g., de-tracking, school-wide positive behavior support systems, looping teachers with the same students over two or more grades, block scheduling, school-within-a-school family-like smaller configurations of learning communities, a Multi-Tiered System of Supports, universal design for learning) are the same best practices that facilitate access and success for students with disabilities. Conversely, special education best practices (e.g., task and concept analysis; structured note taking and cloze procedures; differentiated accommodations and modifications; use of technology and assistive technology to facilitate access to content, products, and learning processes) and English language learning strategies (e.g., use of visual supports, anchor charts, word walls, realia) also facilitate the learning of students perceived as typical or accelerated learners.

Continuous effective planning for installing, expanding, and sustaining an inclusive education vision and set of best practices requires attention to at least five variables: vision, skills, incentives, resources, and action planning (Villa & Thousand 2005; in press). These five variables need to be planned for and revisited periodically for goal and activity adjustment and assessment of the integrity and progress of a school's implementation and sustainability plan. Table 5 describes the actions that need to be taken to forward and sustain an inclusive (or any) education philosophy and practice.

Table 5.
Five Requisite Variables and Associated Actions for Continuous Improvement and Sustainability

Vision
Articulate an inclusive vision and build consensus for that vision.

Skills
Develop educator, administrator, paraeducator, parent, and student knowledge, skills, and confidence for implementing quality inclusive education best practices.

Incentives
Create and implement a menu of meaningful incentives (e.g., extra planning time, professional development opportunities, opportunities to share successes with others) for personnel to take risks and try something new to implement inclusive education.

Resources
Expand and sustain human, technological, fiscal, and organizational resources to implement inclusive education.

Action Planning
Engage in ongoing planning for the process of change.

Complacency — thinking and acting as if you have "arrived" and do not need to tend to a change effort — can be the most harmful barrier to sustaining any change. Complacency can stifle the maintenance of an inclusive schooling vision and quality inclusive practice. Creating inclusive environments is a long-term commitment that requires continuing vigilance. Change agents, no matter what the initiative, must articulate the vision for new staff every year they come on board, provide continuous quality professional development, maintain incentives (e.g., celebrating innovators), provide human and other resource allocations, and engage in ongoing planning and assessment of the quality of inclusive education experiences for everyone.

Inclusive Education
Best Practice Checklist Assessment

Inclusive Education Best Practice #15:
Self-Assessment: Site-Based Continuous Planning for Sustainability

Directions: Based upon your experience, please give each of the following 9 indicators a (zero to 4) rating in response to the question, "To what degree does this indicator occur in my school?"

0	1	2	3	4
Never	Rarely	Some of the time	Most of the time	Always

Rating (0 – 4)	Indicator of Site-Based Continuous Planning for Sustainability
☐	1. Following an assessment of implementation of quality inclusive practices (such as the use of this book), the school *develops, monitors, and updates* goals and activities on a *measurable inclusive education improvement plan at least annually.*
☐	2. The school's *inclusive education improvement plan is based upon an analysis of assessment data* regarding a) the extent to which best practices (e.g., the 15 practices included in this book) are implemented; b) services offered by the school and how they relate to student, family, and community needs; and c) measures of school and post-secondary performance of students, as well as other sources of feedback from school personnel, families, and community partners.
☐	3. The school's inclusive education improvement plan is *widely disseminated* in accessible formats and explained to school personnel, families, students, and community members.

Rating   Indicator of Site-Based Continuous
(0 – 4)   Planning for Sustainability

---

4. The school's inclusive education improvement plan includes strategies to a) *build consensus for the vision* of educating students of mixed-ability in general education settings, b) build *professional capacity* and skills of school personnel to effectively collaborate in planning and teaching, use evidence-based and differentiated instruction methodologies and assessment practices, and c) maintain and enhance *collaboration* with families and community partners.

5. The school's inclusive education improvement plan has *clear and measureable activities and timelines* for improving best practices.

6. The site-based inclusive education improvement plan includes meaningful *incentives* for personnel to take risks to try new things to implement inclusive practices (e.g., professional development, sharing successes at conferences, planning time) and adequate resources (human, technological, fiscal, and organizational) to sustain and expand inclusive education.

7. The site-based inclusive education improvement plan allows for *at least annual adjustments in caseloads* and collaborative teaming and co-teaching *configurations* based upon anticipated student support needs across grades and classes.

8. A *building-based team meets regularly to monitor progress* on implementing the site-based inclusive education improvement plan and to make necessary adjustments in activities and timelines to achieve planned outcomes.

9. A factor considered and assessed during the process of *hiring of new instructional and administrative personnel* is the *candidate's knowledge of and commitment to inclusive education* best practices.

Total Score (out of 36 maximum): _____

Mean Score (Total Score/9): _____

Range of Scores: _____ (low) to   _____ (high)

References

Baker, E., Wang, M. & Wahlberg, H. (1994). The effects of inclusion on learning. *Educational Leadership,* 52(4), 33-35.

Bambara, L.M., Kogen, F., Burns, R. & Singley, D. (2016). Building skills for home and community. In F. Brown, J. McDonnell, & M.E. Snell (Eds.). *Education students with severe disabilities* (8th ed.) (pp. 438 – 473). Boston: Pearson.

Benjamin, S (1989). An ideascape for education: What futurists recommend. *Educational Leadership,* 46(6), 8-14.

Biklen, D. & Burke, J. (2006). Presuming competence. *Equity and Excellence in Education,* 39, 166-176.

Blackorby, J., Wagner, M., Camero, R., Davies, E., Levine, P., Newman, L., Marder, C., & Sumi, C. with Chorost, M., Garza, N., & Guzman, A.M. (2005). *Engagement, academics, social adjustments, and independence.* Palo Alto, CA: Stanford Research Institute. Retrieved from www.seels.net/designdocs/engagement/All_SEELS_outcomes_10-04-05.pdf

California Services for Technical Assistance and Training (2015). A multitiered system of supports with response to intervention and universal design for learning: Putting it all together (Special insert), *The Special EDge,* 28(2), 1-4.

Council for Exceptional Children (1994). Creating schools for all our students: What 12 schools have to say. *Working Forum on Inclusive Schools.* Reston, VA: Author.

Cross, G. & Villa, R. (1992). The Winooski school system: An evolutionary perspective of a school restructuring for diversity. In R. Villa & J. Thousand (Eds.). *Restructuring for caring and effective education: An administrative guide to creating heterogeneous schools* (pp. 219-240). Baltimore, MD: Paul H. Brookes Publishing.

Donnellan, A. (1984). The criterion of the least dangerous assumption. *Behavioral Disorders,* 9, 141-150.

Falvey, M., Blair, M., Dingle, M.P. & Franklin, N. (2000). Creating a community of learners with varied needs. In R. A. Villa & J. S. Thousand (Eds.). *Restructuring for caring and effective education: An administrative guide to creating heterogeneous schools* (2nd ed.), (pp. 186-207). Baltimore, MD: Paul H. Brookes Publishing.

Fox, T. & Williams, W. (1991). *Implementing best practices for all students in their local school.* (Monograph 12-1). Burlington: University of Vermont, Center for Developmental Disabilities.

Gardner, H. (2011). *Frames of mind: The theory of multiple intelligences* (3rd ed.). New York: Basic Books.

Gartner, A., & Lipsky, D.K. (1987). *Beyond special education: Toward a quality education system for all students.* Harvard Educational Review, 57, 367-395.

Giangreco, M. F. (1996). *Vermont interdependent services team approach: A guide to coordinating educational support services.* Baltimore, MD: Paul H. Brookes.

Giangreco, M.F., Cloninger, C.J. & Iverson, V.S. (2011). *Choosing outcomes and accommodations for children (COACH): A guide to educational planning for students with disabilities.* (3rd ed.). Baltimore, MD: Paul H. Brookes.

Giangreco, M.F., Dymond, S.K., Shogren, K.A. (2016). Educating student with severe disabilities: Foundational concept and practices. In F. Brown, J. McDonnell, & M.E. Snell (Eds.) *Instruction of students with severe disabilities* (8th ed.), (1-26). Boston, MA: Pearson.

Giangreco, M. Prelock, P. Reid, R., Dennis, R., & Edelman, S. (2000). Roles of related service personnel in inclusive schools. In R. A. Villa and J. S. Thousand (Eds.). *Restructuring for caring and effective education: Piecing the puzzle together* (2nd ed.), (293-327). Baltimore, MD: Paul H. Brookes.

Gregory, G. & Chapman, C. (2013). *Differentiated instructional strategies: One size does not fit all* (3rd ed.). Thousand Oaks, CA: Corwin Press.

Hall, T., Strangman, N., & Meyer, A. (2011, Winter). *Differentiated instruction and implications for UDL implementation.* Wakefield, MA: National Center on Accessing the General Curriculum.

Halvorsen, A.T., Tweit-Hull, D., Meinders, D., Falvey, M., & Anderson, J. (2004). *Starter kit for inclusive education.* Sacramento, CA: WestEd: LRE Resources Project; and San Diego, CA: SDSU and Hayward, CA: CSUH: Project CLEAR and the California Confederation on Inclusive Education Project.

Individuals with Disabilities Education Improvement Act of 2004, PL 108-17, 20 U.S.C. SS 1400 et seq.

Jorgensen, C. (2005). The least dangerous assumption: A challenge to create a new paradigm. *Disability Solutions,* 6(3), 1 & 5-8.

Kalambouga, A., Farrell, P., & Dyson, A. (2007). The impact of placing pupils with special educational needs in mainstream schools on the achievement of their peers. *Educational Research,* 49(4), 365-382.

Kelly, D. (1992). Introduction. In T. Neary A. Halvorsen, R. Kronberg, & D. Kelly (Eds.). *Curricular adaptations for inclusive classrooms* (pp. 1-6). San Francisco: California Research Institute for the Integration of Students with Severe Disabilities, San Francisco State University.

Lipsky, D., & Gartner, A. (1989). *Beyond separate education: Quality education for all.* Baltimore: Paul H. Brookes.

McNeil, M., Villa, R., & Thousand, J. (1995). Enhancing special education teacher education in Honduras: An international cooperation model. In A. Artiles and D. Hallahan (Eds.). *Special education in Latin America.* Westport, CT: Greenwood Publishing Groups.

National Alternate Assessment Center (2006). *Designing from the ground floor: Alternate assessment on alternate standards. Part three: Theory of learning – What students with the most significant cognitive disabilities should know and be able to do...* (A publication of the U.S. Office of Special Education and Rehabilitative Services.) Retrieved from www.osepideast hatwork.org/toolkit/ground_floor_part_1e.asp

National Center on School Restructuring and Inclusion. (1996). *National study on inclusive education.* New York: City University of New York.

Office of Special Education and Rehabilitative Services (2014). *36th annual report to Congress on the implementation of the Individuals with Disabilities Education Act.* Alexandria, VA: ED PUBS, Education Publications Center, U.S. Department of Education. Retrieved from http://www2.ed.gov/about/reports/annual/osep/2014/parts-b-c/36th-idea-arc.pdf

Ohtake, Y. (2003). Increasing class membership of students with severe disabilities through contribution to classmates' learning. *Research and Practice for Persons with Severe Disabilities, 28,* 228-231.

O'Neill, R.E. & Jameson, J.M. (2016). Designing and implementing individualized positive behavior support. In F. Brown, J. McDonnell, & M.E. Snell (Eds.) *Instruction of students with severe disabilities* (8th ed.), (1-26). Boston, MA: Pearson.

Rainforth, B. & York-Barr (1997). *Collaborative teams for students with severe disabilities: Integrating therapy and educational services* (2nd ed.). Baltimore, MD: Paul H. Brookes.

Rogan, P., Hagner, D., & Murphy, S. (1993). Natural supports: Reconceptualizing job coach roles. *Journal of The Association for Persons with Severe Handicaps, 18,* 275-281.

Schwab Learning (2003). Collaboratively speaking: A study on effective ways to teach children with learning differences in the general education classroom. *The Special EDge, 16*(3), 1-4.

Straub, D. & Peck, C. (1994). What are the outcomes for nondis-
abled students? *Educational Leadership,* 52(4), 36-40.

Sailor, W. & McCart, A. (2014). Stars in alignment. *Research and
Practice for Persons with Severe Disabilities,* 39(1), 55-64.

Shogren, K., McCart, A., Lyon, K., & Sailor, W. (2015). All means
all: Building knowledge for inclusive schoolwide transformation. *Research and Practice for Persons with Severe Disabilities,* 40(3), 173-192.

Snyder, T.D., and Dillow, S.A. (2015). *Digest of Education
Statistics 2013* (NCES 2015-011). National Center for Education
Statistics, Institute of Education Sciences, U.S. Department of
Education. Washington, DC.

Thousand, J., Fox, T., Reid, R., Godek, J. and Williams, W. (1986).
*The homecoming model: Educating students who present
intensive educational challenges within regular education
environments.* (Monograph 7-1). Burlington: University of
Vermont, Center for Developmental Disabilities.

Thousand, J., Villa, R., & Nevin, A. (2015). *Differentiating instruction: Planning for universal design and teaching for college
and career readiness* (2nd ed.). Thousand Oaks, CA: Corwin
Press.

United States Department of Education. (1995). *Seventeenth
annual report to Congress on the implementation of the
Individuals with Disabilities Education Act.* Washington, DC:
Author.

Universal Design for Learning (2013). What it is, what it looks
like, where to learn more. *The Special EDge,* 26(1), 2-3.

Villa, R., Falvey, M., & Schrag, J. (2003). System change in Los
Angeles: The city of angels. In D. Fisher and N. Frey (Eds.).
Inclusive urban schools. Baltimore: MD: Paul H. Brookes.

Villa, R., Keefe, L., Jarry, E., & Del Rosario, B. (2003). *Least restrictive environment (LRE) assessment and planning tool.* Santa
Fe, NM: New Mexico State Department of Education.

Villa, R., Martinez, S., Keefe, L., Garcia, R., Hendrix, B., and Gallegos, A. (2005). *New Mexico's LRE initiative: A collaboratively developed and implemented systems change plan.* Paper presented at TASH conference, The Heart of TASH — 30 Years and Still Beating Strong. Milwaukee, WI, November 9-12.

Villa, R., Tac, L.V., Muc, P.M., Ryan, S., Thuy, N.T.M., Weil, C., &Thousand, J. (2003). Inclusion in Vietnam: A decade of implementation. *Research and Practice for Persons with Severe Disabilities,* 28(1), 23-32.

Villa, R. & Thousand, J. (1996, March). *Assembly: Preservice and inservice personnel preparation to support the inclusion of children with disabilities in general education classrooms.* Paper presented at Association for Supervision and Curriculum Development Annual Conference, New Orleans, LA.

Villa, R. & Thousand, J. (2003). Lessons learned from more than 20 years of research and practice in developing and sustaining inclusive education in developed and developing nations. In M.L.H. Hui, C. Robin Dowson, and M. Gonzles Moont (Eds.). *Inclusive education in the new millennium.* Hong Kong and Macau: Education Convergence and the Association for Childhood Education International.

Villa, R. & Thousand, J. (2005). *Creating an inclusive school* (2nd ed.). Alexandria, VA: Association for Supervision and Curriculum Development.

Villa, R. & Thousand, J. (2011). *RTI: Co-teaching and differentiated instruction.* Port Chester, NY: National Professional Resources.

Villa, R. & Thousand, J. (2012). *Quality education practices assessment.* San Diego, CA: Bayridge Consortium Incorporated.

Villa, R. & Thousand, J. (in press). *Leading the inclusive school.* Alexandria, VA: Association for Supervision and Curriculum Development.

Villa, R. & Thousand, J., & Nevin, A. (2010). *Collaborating with students in instruction and decision making: The untapped resource.* Thousand Oaks, CA: Corwin Press.

Villa, R., Thousand, J., & Nevin, A. (2013). *A guide to co-teaching: New lessons and strategies to facilitate student learning* (3rd ed.). Thousand Oaks, CA: Corwin Press.

Villa, R., Thousand, J., Nevin, A., & Meyers, H. (1996). Teacher and administrator perceptions of heterogeneous education. *Exceptional Children,* 63(1), pp. 29-45.

Willis, S. & Mann, L. (2000, Winter). *Curriculum Update. News letter for the Association for Supervision and Curriculum Development.* Alexandria, VA: Association for Supervision and Curriculum Development.

Wilson, G.L., & Michaels, C.A. (2006). General and special education students' perceptions of co-teaching: Implications for secondary-level literacy instruction. *Reading & Writing Quarterly: Overcoming Learning Difficulties,* 22(3), 205-225.